25

# T
# WES
# ISLES

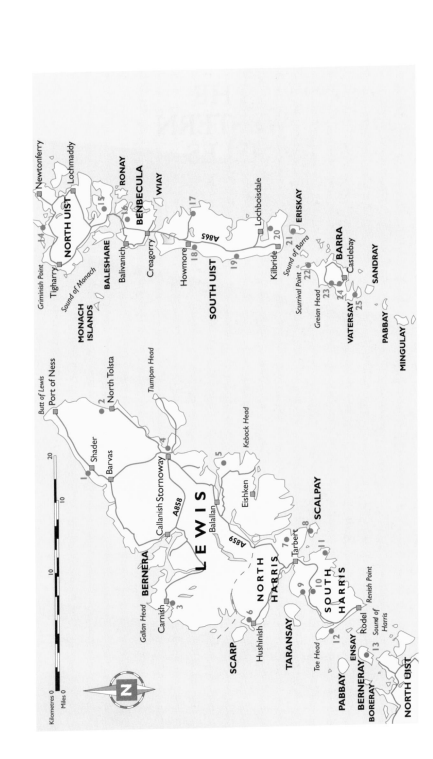

## 25 WALKS

# THE WESTERN ISLES

**June Parker**

Series Editor: Roger Smith

WESTERN ISLES
TOURIST BOARD

Western Isles Tourism Development Programme

**EDINBURGH:HMSO**

First published 1996

HMSO Scotland
South Gyle Crescent
Edinburgh EH12 9EB

Applications for reproduction should be made to HMSO

### Acknowledgements

Special thanks are due to Susan Maclennan of the Western Isles Tourism
Development Programme for much help and advice in the preparation of this
book, and for providing some of the illustrations for Walks 5 and 10.
Thanks are also due to James Smith for providing two of the illustrations for Walk 5.

The author would also like to thank the following for providing information and
for helpful comments on the text:

Rhoda Campbell, Barra Historical Society
Helen McDonald, Southern Isles Amenity Trust
Gill Maclean, Open University
David Maclennan, Area Officer for Lewis and Harris, Scottish Natural Heritage
Alisdair MacInnes, South Lochboisdale
Calum MacRitchie, Pairc Historical Society
Dolina Macleod, Western Isles Council

The publishers have followed the recommendations of the
Scottish Examination Board in the spelling of Gaelic words.

All facts have been checked as far as possible but the author and publishers
cannot be held responsible for any errors, however caused.

British Library Cataloguing in Publication Data

A catalogue record for this book is available from the British Library

ISBN 0 11 495740 1

# CONTENTS

# USEFUL INFORMATION

The length of each walk is given in kilometres and miles, but within the text measurements are metric for simplicity. The walks are described in detail and are supported by accompanying maps (study them before you start the walk), so there is little likelihood of getting lost, but if you want a backup you will find the Ordnance Survey 1:50,000 maps on sale locally. In fact if you intend to do any hillwalking, including several of the walks in this book, then these maps are essential. The 1:25,000 Pathfinder series are not available on the islands, except in Stornoway.

Every care has been taken to make the descriptions and maps as accurate as possible, but the author and publishers can accept no responsibility for errors, however caused. Most of the walks in this book are not on 'official' or maintained paths, and neither the publisher nor the landowners can be held responsible for any accident, however caused.

The countryside is always changing and there will inevitably be alterations to some aspects of these walks as time goes by. The publishers and author would be happy to receive comments and suggested alterations for future editions of the book.

## Ordnance Survey

The OS is the national mapping agency, covering the whole of the UK at various scales. The two most frequently used by walkers are 1:25,000 and 1:50,000. All OS maps are drawn on a grid of kilometre squares. The Western Isles are covered by 6 sheets in the 1:50,000 Landranger series as follows:

8, Stornoway & North Lewis.
13, West Lewis & North Harris.
14, Tarbert & Loch Seaforth.
18, Sound of Harris & St.Kilda.
22, Benbecula.
31, Barra & surrounding Islands.

## Hill walking

Many of the walks in this book are on good tracks and paths at sea level, and these can be walked in trainers.

---

### METRIC MEASUREMENTS

At the beginning of each walk, the distance is given in miles and kilometres. Within the text, all measurements are metric for simplicity (and indeed our Ordnance Survey maps are now all metric). However, it was felt that a conversion table might be useful to those readers who still tend to think in Imperial terms.

The basic statistic to remember is that one kilometre is five-eighths of a mile. Half a mile is equivalent to 800 metres and a quarter-mile is 400 metres. Below that distance, yards and metres are little different in practical terms.

| km | miles |
|----|-------|
| 1 | 0.625 |
| 1.6 | 1 |
| 2 | 1.25 |
| 3 | 1.875 |
| 3.2 | 2 |
| 4 | 2.5 |
| 4.8 | 3 |
| 5 | 3.125 |
| 6 | 3.75 |
| 6.4 | 4 |
| 7 | 4.375 |
| 8 | 5 |
| 9 | 5.625 |
| 10 | 6.25 |
| 16 | 10 |

Only three of the walks in this book go higher than 500m, but some of the lower level walks traverse rough and pathless ground, and it is recommended that walkers should be properly equipped with warm and waterproof clothing, including good boots, and be competent in the use of map and compass. There are many more mountain walks throughout the Western Isles which are beyond the scope and space available in this book, particularly in North Harris. Please ensure that wherever you walk, details of your route are left with someone.

**Other walks**

The Western Isles Tourism Development Programme is publishing a series of leaflets about walks which are most informative on the history and wildlife of the area. Some of these routes are waymarked. These leaflets are available from all the tourist information centres.

**Travel information**

There are regular ferry crossings from the mainland by several routes:

Oban to Castlebay (Barra) and Lochboisdale (South Uist).
Uig (Skye) to Lochmaddy (North Uist) and Tarbert (Harris).
Ullapool to Stornoway.

For details of timetables and fares contact Caledonian Macbrayne, The Ferry Terminal, Gourock PA19 1QB (01475 650100). For ferry bookings phone 01475 650000 (Mon-Sat, 0830–1700).

By air, British Airways offer direct flights to Stornoway from both Glasgow and Inverness. These flights operate up to three times daily from Monday to Saturday. There is also a daily flight (not Sundays) from Glasgow to Benbecula. British Airways Express also offer daily flights from Glasgow to Barra (where the plane lands on the beach!). Additional Sunday flights are scheduled in summer.

Regular inter-island flights connecting Stornoway, Benbecula and Barra are operated by British Airways Express. For reservations phone British Airways on 0345 222 111.

**Getting about on the islands**

Public transport is of limited use to the visitor, except for the regular service between Tarbert and Stornoway. Most visitors take their own cars, but there are car hire facilities available on the islands. Cycling is popular and there are bicycle hire centres too. Visitors for the first time may find single-track roads alarming to begin with, but there is no problem if speeds are kept low and you pull in to passing places to allow overtaking. A polite handwave to other drivers is customary.

## Gaelic language

At present most of the signposts are in Gaelic, although in 1995 a decision was taken by the Islands Council to introduce dual language signs. This will take some time to implement, so until then an OS map with anglicised names is a help in finding your way around. The official Tourist Map, which has Gaelic and English names, is also recommended.

## Country/Crofting code

Walkers are welcome almost everywhere in the Western Isles, but it is essential that the country code is followed meticulously.

* Avoid damaging crops;
* Try to avoid crossing fences;
* Leave gates as you find them, and be especially careful to close any gate you have to open;
* Never drop litter, and if possible pick up litter which others have carelessly discarded;
* Respect the life and work of the countryside;
* Keep dogs under control at all times and on a leash near livestock;
* Park your car without blocking access for others;
* Do not disturb breeding birds;
* Protect wildlife and plants;
* Avoid damaging archaeological sites.

## Western Isles Tourist Board

The main office in Stornoway is open all year, the others are seasonal opening from Easter to early October. All offices open late for ferry arrivals.

*Tourist Information Centres:*
* Lewis: 26 Cromwell Street, Stornoway, Isle of Lewis HS1 2DD (01851 703088).
* Harris: Pier Road, Tarbert (01859 502011).
* North Uist: Pier Road, Lochmaddy (01876 500321).
* South Uist: Pier Road, Lochboisdale (01878 700286).
* Barra: Main Street, Castlebay (01871 810336).

## Accommodation

A brochure listing hotels, guest houses, bed and breakfast and self-catering accommodation is available from the Western Isles Tourist Board. There are few official campsites, but it is often possible to get permission to pitch a small tent. The non-profit-making Gatliff Trust provides a number of simple hostels in out-of-the-way places, charging the same as SYHA grade 3 hostels. Each is looked after by a local warden. These are at:

* Na Gearrannan (Garenin) on West Lewis.
* Tobha Mòr (Howmore) on South Uist.
* Reinigeadal (Rhenigidale).
* Eilean Bhearnaraigh (the island of Berneray).
* There is an SYHA hostel at Loch nam Madadh (Lochmaddy) and at Stocinis on Harris.

> IT IS HOPED THAT THERE WILL BE A GATLIFF HOSTEL OPENED IN BREVIG, BARRA IN 1997.

## Sunday Observance

This is very strict on Lewis and Harris. All shops and petrol stations are closed on Sundays, and most are closed on the other islands too. Many of the ferries do not run on Sundays. Make sure you are stocked up with essentials on Saturday and it will not affect your holiday. On Lewis and Harris most hotel bars and pubs are also closed, and some bed and breakfast places prefer it if guests book ahead (on the Saturday) for Sunday nights.

Sunday observance is a very important part of island life, especially on Lewis and Harris; please respect it. If you are going for a walk on a Sunday you will need to get any food or drink you need the day before.

# INTRODUCTION

The Western Isles, better known to the outside world as the Outer Hebrides and sometimes also as the Long Island, are a chain of islands about 210km (130 miles) long and lying between 50-100km (30-60 miles) from the north-west coast of Scotland. The total population of the ten inhabited islands is just under 30,000, nearly all of them living in small crofting communities except for the one town of Stornoway in Lewis. This is the administrative capital and has about 8000 inhabitants.

The islands are renowned for superb scenery which includes beaches of silver or golden shell sand washed by seas bright with jewel colours of amethyst, turquoise and sapphire and a pale luminous green where the sand shows through. There are rugged mountains as wild as any on the mainland with the bare backbone of ancient gneiss outcropping among the heather and peat of the moorland.

On the west coasts there is the unique machair, where blown shell sand produces a lime-rich soil that supports a profusion of wild flowers and is cultivated by the crofter to grow crops for animal food. There are myriads of lochs and lochans and a coastline with rocky cliffs and inlets. The whole area is a paradise for naturalists and birdwatchers. Ecologically, the area is important because of its position at the extreme western edge of Europe, and there are 40 Sites of Special Scientific Interest. Scottish Natural Heritage has identified 40% of the land area as being of outstanding scenic value. In addition there are many archaeological sites throughout the islands including prehistoric forts, chambered cairns and the Stone Circle at Callanish, which is of international importance.

The walks in this book have been chosen to include as many distinctive features of the islands as possible. They vary in length from 4 to 15 km (2½ to 9 miles) and none of them is especially arduous. In the case of the longer walks, shorter versions are suggested whenever possible. Equally, possibilities of longer walks are indicated when appropriate. Some of the hill walks are pathless, and because of the nature of the land may involve picking a way through boggy ground. All the walks are within the scope of the average fit person. Times are given for guidance only, and although generous do not include rest stops.

The sunniest weather is in May and June and the driest months are from May to August, but days without wind are rare. Even when it seems cold because of the wind, the sun is liable to burn and it is wise to use protective creams. Lightweight waterproof and windproof outer clothing should be taken and strong waterproof boots are advised for many walks. Although a map is provided for each walk, the appropriate OS Landranger map is listed as these provide invaluable information and interest. They are also a help in finding the starting point of the walks and in identifying distant landmarks. The Western Isles are covered by six of these maps and they are all available locally. (See information section.)

The Western Isles are a unique corner of the British Isles, different in many ways from the Inner Hebrides and even more different from the mainland. They have a different culture, language and scenery and are much more sparsely populated, yet each island has its own individual character. I hope you enjoy these walks as much as I have done and equally enjoy the discovery of the special charms of the individual islands.

JUNE PARKER

Opposite: Replica of Rune Stone, Chille Barra

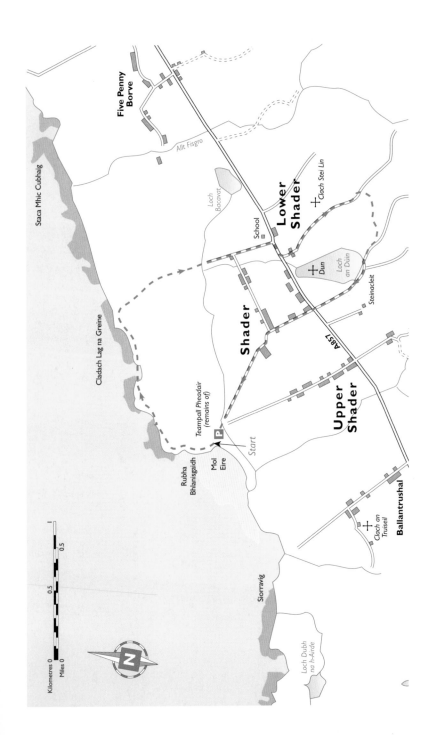

# STEINACLEIT:
# A NEOLITHIC MONUMENT

## INFORMATION

**Distance:** 6½ km (4 miles).

**Map:** OS Landranger sheet 8, Stornoway and North Lewis.

**Start and finish:** Leave the A857 at Siadar Uarach (Upper Shader) and drive down to the road end, where there is parking space outside a fenced area by the coast.

**Terrain:** All easy walking on roads and tracks with a short section on grass. No special footwear needed.

**Time:** Allow about 2 hours.

**Opening hours:** *Arnol Blackhouse:* open all year. Phone 01851 710395 to check exact times and admission charges.

Lewis has been inhabited for over 5000 years, and the landscape in the north-west of the island reveals many facets of the life of man during this long span of time. The people who lived here made many marks on the landscape, leaving burial mounds and standing great stones on end. One of the earliest and perhaps most impressive are the standing stones, of which those at Calanais (Callanish) are the best known. Around 2000 years ago, fortifications were built such as the great fort or Broch at Carlabhagh (Carloway) and many smaller duns on islands or headlands where people could keep themselves safe. With the coming of Christianity, places of worship were built. All this and more is seen during this walk.

The Steinacleit site has not been excavated or dated, so its function and age are uncertain. Once thought to be a chambered burial cairn surrounded by standing stones, it is now interpreted as a domestic settlement, although it may have been used for different purposes over a long period of time. Although the site is not particularly impressive to look at, a visit is well worth while. The central mound is overlain by a large oval foundation which is thought to have been a house or hall. Other walls, possibly old field walls, disappear away under the peat. The site is on a low hill overlooking a small loch on which is a dun, reached by a causeway. The standing stone Clach Stei Lin lies about 500m to the north-east.

Other points of interest include the foundations of the ruined Teampall Pheadair, dating from the early Christian period. The whole of this area has evidence of the more recent past in the large number of ruined black houses. At Arnol, one has been restored and opened as a museum. Although this house was built in 1885, it was designed and constructed according to methods in use for the last 1000 years. The house is

Clach an Truiseil.

built in one unit with cattle housed in a byre at one end, in order to utilise heat given off by the cattle. This house was lived in until 1964 and still has the original box beds. The fragrant but rather acrid smoke from the central peat fire which burns every day conjures up the genuine atmosphere of the past, and a visit is strongly recommended.

To start the walk, leave the track and walk along the grass above the rocky foreshore to the remains of the temple. All that can be seen is a rectangular area about 11 m long. On the low cliff face of the nearby point, Rubha Bhlanisgaidh, midden material including pottery, seashells and animal bones can be seen and probably indicate occupation from the late Iron Age to the medieval period. Continue along the grass outside the fenced land. This walk northwards along the coast is particularly good for observing waders such as redshanks and oystercatchers as well as moorland birds like golden plovers.

Keep on by the coast, where vehicles have made a rough track along the grass. After passing some rusty abandoned machinery there is a stile over a cross fence. Turn right after crossing the stile and head diagonally inland to a dyke or turf-covered wall. Follow this up to the corner of a fence and go through the narrow gate, then walk up by the fence to join a track at a right-angled bend. This same point could be reached from Teampall Pheadair by walking up the rough track from there, passing on the way a large number of ruined buildings. Follow the track inland to the main road at Lower Shader (Siadar) where there is a school on the corner.

Turn right and after 100 m turn left along a narrow lane leading towards a small plantation. Take a left fork and continue along the lane until level with the trees, where a gate on the left gives access to the standing stone Clach Stei Lin. This stone is on the perimeter of a large circle of low grass-covered stones; at the opposite point on the circle a large monolith lies fallen.

Return to the gate. From here Steinacleit can be seen on the hill to the south-west, but cannot be reached directly. Turn left along the track until a narrow wooden gate is found at a bend. Go through this and walk along by the fence for a short distance to reach a

Steinacleit.

place where it can be stepped over without difficulty. Cross the grass to the Steinacleit site.

From the site there is an overview of Siadar, a small crofting township typical of others on this coastal strip. The land slopes fairly gently to the sea and there is little machair compared with the west coasts further south along the island chain. All the same, it supports a fair population compared with the interior, which is an uninhabitable peat bog known as the Black Moor. The Black Moor has a deep covering of peat which has accumulated over 9000 years and this provides an invaluable source of fuel for the people living on the coastal fringe. Cattle and sheep can be grazed in summer on some of the ground, especially when the peat has been stripped, leaving an exposure of boulder clay. With some reseeding and the application of shell sand and seaweed, this 'skimmed ground' can become good soil. The Black Moor is scattered with summer shielings.

To complete the circuit, descend to the access gate near Loch an Duin. Walk to the main road and go straight across, turning left then right in the village of Siadar.

In the area of this walk at Siadar there is an impressive monolith, Clach an Truiseil, which at 5.7 m in height is the largest in the North of Scotland. It can readily be visited either before or after the walk in a short diversion from the main road at the village of Baile an Truiseil (Ballantrushal).

Loch an Dùin from Steinacleit.

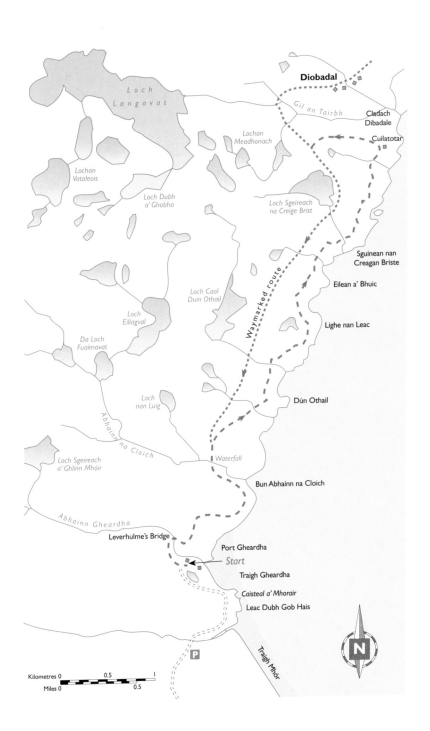

Loch
Langavat

Diobadal

Gil an Tairbh

Cladach
Dibadale

Lochan
Meadhonach

Cuilatotar

Lochan
Vataleois

Loch Dubh
a' Ghobha

Loch Sgeireach
na Creige Brist

Sguinean nan
Creagan Briste

Waymarked route

Eilean a' Bhuic

Loch Caol
Duin Othail

Lighe nan Leac

Loch
Eillagval

Da Loch
Fuaimavat

Dùn Othail

Loch
nan Luig

Abhainn na Cloich

Loch Sgeireach
a' Ghlinn Mhóir

Waterfall

Bun Abhainn na Cloich

Abhainn Gheardha

Leverhulme's Bridge

Port Gheardha

*Start*

Traigh Gheardha

Caisteal a' Mhorair

Leac Dubh Gob Hais

Traigh Mhór

**P**

Kilometres 0      0.5      1
Miles 0      0.5

N

# TRAIGH GHEARDHA TO DIOBADAL

This clifftop walk on the east coast of Lewis is ideal for getting away from it all. The coastal scenery is dramatic, with detached sea stacks and rocky islands where seals can be seen basking, huge landslip features and cliffs where in early summer every ledge is crammed with nesting fulmars, cormorants and kittiwakes. You may see skuas, or even a golden eagle. On the cliff tops there are many orchids and among the heather on the moorland there are patches of bright blue milkwort, yellow tormentil and deep pink lousewort. The pale green leaves and violet flowers of butterwort brighten the damp places.

There is no road on this part of the coast, but the route partly follows the planned route of a road started by Lord Leverhulme in the 1920s. This was never completed, but the bridge he built over the Abhainn Gheardha (Garry River, spelt Geiraha on some OS maps) remains a historic landmark. A waymarked route has now been made covering the 16km (10 miles) between Sgiogarstaigh (Skigersta) in the north and Traigh Gheardha in the south, passing through the old shieling village of Diobadal (Dibadale, pronounced Jibadel with the accent on the first syllable). This is a linear walk that can be done by parties with two cars, but that involves an exceedingly long drive to retrieve the second car. At the time of writing there is talk of this walk becoming the first stage in a new long distance route, the Hebridean Way.

A short and easy alternative walk is to visit the waterfall on the Abhainn na Cloich (river of stones). Although the falls can be seen from the road, the best views are to be had by crossing the concrete bridge and going down the bank on the other side of the river. (4km or 2.5 miles for the return trip). This may leave time to explore the small attractive beach at Geardha (Garry) where there are stacks and caves accessible at

## INFORMATION

**Distance:** 15 km (9 miles).

**Map:** OS Landranger sheet 8, Stornoway and North Lewis.

**Start and finish:** Garry beach car park, signposted Traigh Gheiraha. Drive north from Stornoway on the A857 and take the right fork on B895 at Newmarket. Continue through North Tolsta and New Tolsta and past the car park for Traigh Mhor.

**Terrain:** Easy walking on the unfinished road to the waterfall on the Abhainn na Cloich, then mainly pathless and boggy moorland except for some grassy sheep tracks near the cliff edge. Boots essential. Take great care near the cliff edges.

**Time:** There are several ups and downs and the going is rough so allow about 5 hours.

**Toilets:** Available at Traigh Mhor car park.

low tide. For further information on the wildlife and history of this area, see the excellent leaflet Tolstadh-Nis produced by the Western Isles Tourism Development Programme.

From the car park, walk up the hill and cross the bridge. This 'bridge to nowhere' is a substantial affair very much ahead of its time and, surprisingly, wide enough for two cars. Enjoy the easy walking as the good track winds round the headland with fine views back to Garry beach and to the long stretch of golden sands (Traigh Mor, big beach) extending almost to Tolsta Head. When the concrete slab over the Abhainn na Cloich is crossed, follow the route of the projected road for a further 100m until it begins to bend left, then leave it and aim for one of the new yellow-topped green posts on a high mound ahead.

Dun Othail.

When this is reached, bear right and head for the coast to see the dramatic Dun Othail. This is a sea-stack almost separated from the mainland by a deep ravine known as MacNicol's Leap. From this point on follow the coastline to the north, often on sheep tracks which walkers are gradually converting into a fairly continuous path. It winds in and out and up and down so that progress is slow, but about 1km beyond Dun Othail you can look forward to a sudden dramatic view down a steep gully to a bay with rocky stacks and islets.

Continue along the cliff edge, making use of sheep tracks wherever possible. When the rocky island

Eilean Glas Cuilatotar comes into view, make for a ruin next to a rocky outcrop on a patch of bright green grass. This place is known as Cuilatotar. Here are the remains of the house of John Macdonald, who in his youth was press-ganged into the Seaforth Highlanders. When he was released in the 1820s there was no land available for him, so he settled here to enjoy the peace and solitude.

It is a beautiful situation with views down to the sea where seals can be seen basking on the rocks and heard to sing. This makes an excellent spot to rest before retracing your steps back along the cliff edge. A modern bothy can be seen across the ravine. Beyond are the ruined houses of Upper Diobadal, once used as summer shielings. Diobadal is a Norse name meaning 'deep valley'. It looks tempting to go further, but it is rough walking and a long way back, so promise yourself to walk in from the north on some future occasion instead.

If you opt to return by the waymarked moorland route instead of retracing your steps, go inland from the

Looking north along the coast.

ruined house up gently rising ground and look for the green and yellow posts. There is no path, but the posts mark the easiest way through the boggy ground. The way first makes for the seaward side of Loch Sgeireach na Creige Brist, an attractive loch renowned for large but elusive brown trout. The route then swings southwest and continues parallel to the coast, keeping below Loch Caol Duin Othail. Towards the end the direction is southward, to reach the concrete slab over the river and the easy walk back along the track to Garry beach.

# UIG SANDS AND CARNAIS

The extensive white sandy beach near Timsgearraidh (Timsgarry) in West Lewis is rightly famed for its beauty. Backed by high dunes and surrounded by rugged hills, it is a popular spot for local people and visitors alike. The Carnais (Carnish) peninsula to the south is less well known and offers attractions of a different kind, the green turf bright with primroses in late spring. At the northern end a number of rocky islets with shallow water between them are a good area for seabirds, with many cormorants and even some divers if you are lucky. Ringed plovers and dunlin are everywhere. This walk makes almost a circuit of the bay in two sections, both of which require low tide.

In 1831 the walrus ivory 'Lewis chessmen' were found when a sandbank was disturbed at Eadar dha Fhadhail (Ardroil). There were 78 pieces from about 4 incomplete sets and they are dated at about AD1150. Most of these beautifully carved pieces are now in the British Museum and some are in Edinburgh. In the summer of 1995 they were on display in the new museum in Stornoway, and local people feel strongly that some of the collection should be on permanent loan in the islands.

From the grassy car park, cross the sand in a northerly direction to a footbridge over a river channel. To your right are the remains of Dun Borranish dating from the Iron Age period. In early summer the low cliffs are dotted with pink cushions of moss campion. Walk along the grass near the coast to a cottage, then turn left along a small stony beach. Take to the grass again below the wall of the old burial ground of Baile na Cille. Keep on by the edge of the land round a small peninsula (the standard route crosses the peninsula along a wide

## INFORMATION

**Distance:** 13½ km (8½ miles). In two sections, 5 km and 8½ km.

**Map:** OS Landranger sheet 13, West Lewis and North Harris.

**Start and finish:** Leave Stornoway on A859, turn right on A858, then left on B8011 to Timsgearraidh (Timsgarry). Go past Timsgearraidh and continue through Ardroil, taking the 3rd turn right signposted 'To the shore'. Go through a gate and park on the grass.

**Terrain:** Easy walking on sand, grass and narrow lanes. There are two river channels to paddle which can be crossed dryshod if wearing boots and when the tide is low.

**Time:** Allow 4 hours or more (1½ and 2½ hours).

**Toilets:** By the campsite.

Uig sands from Crowlista crossing.

Suainaval from Carnais.

grassy strip between two fences, and this is the route of return). Now cross the sand and ford the river channel to a broad peninsula. Keep round the edge of this, outside the fence, until you come to an old narrow gate which is easily stepped over.

Go over rising ground by a walled area and then drop down to a gate opening on to the road near a group of houses. Turn right and follow the road as far as a small house, opposite which a wide gate gives access to the estuary and the standard route across the river channel. Start crossing the sands, keeping to the right of a low rocky outcrop in the sand and then heading for the grass strip which leads over the headland and back to the coast. Retrace your steps back over the bridge and to the car park to begin the second part of the walk.

Start the next part of the walk to the Carnais peninsula by walking along the sand at the edge of the dunes. A rocky point juts out into the bay at one place and if the tide is in you may have to take to the dunes to get round this. Otherwise simply follow the sand next to the dunes. As the bridge over the Abhainn Caslavat is approached, go up onto the grass outside the fenced area. Cross the bridge and follow the narrow road round to Carnais, passing a large sand and gravel deposit which is being extracted on the site of a glacial ester.

Access to the peninsula is below a house on the right, after passing a large concrete base at the edge of the quarried area. Follow sheep tracks over the grassy headland to the far end with fine views over the small islands. Keep going around the headland for a view of the pretty Carnais Bay from the sandhills, then return to the road by walking around the eastern edge of the headland, enjoying fine views over the sands to the hills of West Lewis. When the river bridge is reached either continue along the narrow road to the starting point, or if preferred and the tide is out, retrace your steps back along the sands.

Carnais Bay.

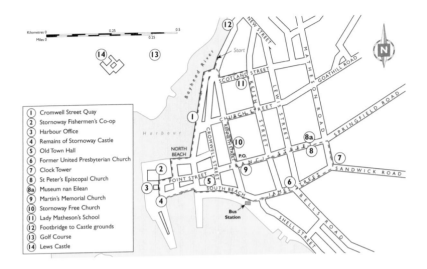

1. Cromwell Street Quay
2. Stornoway Fishermen's Co-op
3. Harbour Office
4. Remains of Stornoway Castle
5. Old Town Hall
6. Former United Presbyterian Church
7. Clock Tower
8. St Peter's Episcopal Church
8a. Museum nan Eilean
9. Martin's Memorial Church
10. Stornoway Free Church
11. Lady Matheson's School
12. Footbridge to Castle grounds
13. Golf Course
14. Lews Castle

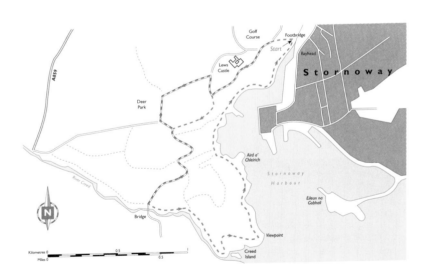

# STORNOWAY AND LEWS CASTLE

## A. *Stornoway Town*

The only major town in the Hebrides, Stornoway has a population of about 8000 (1995) and is a thriving and bustling port. It has a fine natural harbour, which is the centre of the local fishing industry as well as the ferry terminal for sailings to and from Ullapool. Stornoway has no really old buildings in spite of its long history, because they have been cleared to make way for new developments. The oldest house dates from about 1790. This short walk around the town passes several points of interest.

Walk along the Cromwell Street Quay. This is a working harbour with colourful fishing boats, nets and tackle and a view across to Lews Castle. Turn right along North Beach to look at the Stornoway Fisherman's Co-op, one of the oldest buildings in town. Go down Quay Street and turn right then left, passing the Harbour Office on the corner. The remains of Stornoway Castle, once a stronghold of the MacLeod clan, are a pile of rubble below the west pier of the ferry terminal. The castle was dismantled by English soldiers in 1653. Walk along South Beach passing the Town Hall, built at the beginning of the century and restored in 1928 after fire damage. The Art Gallery 'An Lanntair' is housed here.

Continue past the bus station and turn left into James Street. The elaborate building where electrical goods are sold was once the United Presbyterian Church. Continue along James Street to Matheson Road, passing this to look at the Clock Tower, which is all that remains of the original Nicolson Institute school buildings, opened in 1873. Walk up Matheson Road and after passing Garden Road turn left into Francis Street to arrive at St Peter's Episcopal Church.

## INFORMATION

**A. *Stornoway Town***

**Distance:** 2½ km (under 2 miles).

**Start and finish:** Park on the right hand side of the road on Bayhead near the entrance to the town centre (Or join the route at the bus station).

**Terrain:** All pavement.

**Time:** Less than one hour.

**B. *Lews Castle Grounds***

**Distance:** 6 km (4 miles).

**Start and finish:** On Bayhead as for Walk 4(a)

**Terrain:** All easy walking on paths and tracks.

**Time:** Less than 2 hours, but you could spend much longer here exploring other paths.

Stornoway from the Castle grounds.

This is a simple, attractive building set in a tiny garden with, in spring, bluebells below mature trees and shrubs.

Keep straight on along Francis Street to the corner of Kenneth Street, where the large Martin's Memorial Church presides over a busy precinct. Turn right up Kenneth Street, passing the Stornoway Free Church set back on the right. Turn right into Church Street and left into Keith Street to view on the next corner a building which was put up by Lady Matheson in 1848 as a female industrial school. Now divided into two flats, there is an inscription high up on the front facade. Turn left into Scotland Street and right to return to Bayhead where the walk into the Castle grounds begins by the footbridge.

### B. *Lews Castle Grounds*

Lews Castle from Stornoway harbour.

Lews Castle, which stands in extensive grounds, was built by Sir James Matheson, who bought Lewis in 1844. Lord Leverhulme purchased the island in 1918. He eventually gifted the parish of Stornoway to the Town Council and is now administered by the Stornoway Trust. At one time the castle was used as a college, but at the time of writing it is not in use, as extensive and costly repairs are needed to make it safe. One suggested use for the future is to establish a National Gaelic Archive there.

The park-like castle grounds are open to the public and provide delightful walks. The mature trees and lush growth, so rare in the Western Isles, are due to the plantings made by the Mathesons using imported soil, and include some 70 species of mixed conifers and broadleaves with shrubs below. Woodland flowers grow below the shrubs and the tree canopy supports many birds. This varied walk includes mature woodland, open moorland, the beautiful River Creed and views across the harbour to the town.

Cross the footbridge and go up the steps ahead. The path goes into a mature beechwood, through which the open green of the golf course can be seen on the right. Join the road briefly and then fork left over a bridge. Pass in front of the castle, where notices warn against going too close. At the end of the building, cross the grass diagonally right to a narrow path leading below a copper beech and on to an open space with a high Acuparia on the left near a curious granite pillar supporting a steel ball.

Mature trees in the Castle grounds.

The path curves right to a gate with a gap in the adjoining fence. Go up to the seat on the road and turn right, then make a sharp turn left just before reaching another seat. The path climbs steadily to reach some open ground with banks of rhododendrons, after which it descends steeply to a pinewood. Turn left at a T-junction, going past an open area of moorland on the right and meeting a road at another T-junction. Turn left again and after 100 m, turn right by a mature beech and some new plantings. Ignore a left turn. A little further on, ignore some tempting steps on the left, which lead through a muddy tunnel of rhododendrons to a hilltop where the view is obscured by trees.

Continue along the road with a hill on the left. Go right at a T-junction and then take a right fork to reach a bridge over the River Creed. (Those who would like to extend this walk can do so here by crossing the bridge and following the track out to Arnish Point and back.) Turn left and follow the river downstream, passing a memorial fountain and later on a stone shelter with picnic tables. River and road pass through a gorge where the rock walls are festooned with ferns and moss and with bright yellow gorse and broom flowering on the banks, to be followed by massed rhododendrons.

Keep following the road down to the mouth of the Creed. The track then rises inland before turning right to reach the coast again by a panoramic viewpoint with seats. Continue along the track by the sea to return to the footbridge, and so back to the start point.

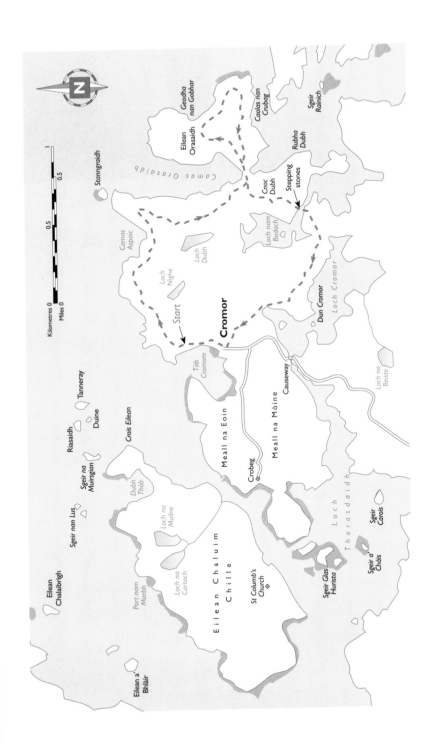

# CROMOR AND EILEAN ORASAIDH

romor is a headland on the east side of Lewis, south of Loch Erisort. It is a remote area, once more easily reached by sea, and was a staging post for the mails to South Lochs before the roads were made drivable. The mails arrived from Crosbost on the north side of Loch Erisort. Fishing was once the main industry in the village, which in 1928/9 had 7 large boats and about 20 smaller ones in the fleet. There was a curing station and salt house on the foreshore over 100 years ago.

The headland is surprisingly rough and wild with rocky outcrops, gullies and cliffs with nesting seabirds and views of uninhabited islands. There is a dun on Loch Cromor and away to the west are the ruins of St Columba's church on a tidal island, Eilean Chaluim Chille.

Unfortunately, there is little now left of Dun Cromor, which was a galleried dun or broch, with a wide staircase of 17 steps within the southern wall, leading to an upper gallery. The causeway connecting the dun to the shore is still visible under the water. Galleried duns like this were built throughout the islands some 2000 years ago.

Eilean Chaluim Chille was once an important centre of religion, being cited in a report of 1549 as the main place of worship for the parish of Lochs. There was probably a church there from about 800AD, built by

Small islands at Cromor.

the followers of St Columba, who died on Iona in 597AD. The cemetery was in use until 1878. The island can be reached, at low tide only, by a causeway from Crobeg. This is a short and interesting excursion which could be made after the main walk.

From the village, continue along the lane past a house and then turn right up a steep track. Go through the second gate on the left and follow traces of an old path along the high ground and between two fenced areas. When a rocky top comes into view with a loch below it, drop down to the valley at the seaward side by zig-zagging down the grassy slope, which is quite steep. Then ascend the ridge running out towards Stanngraidh by a thin path sloping up diagonally above the steep rocky ground below. Once the ridge is reached, turn right and follow the high ground over the 73m top. (Do not try to find a way along the east coast near sea level; there is a section of impassable cliff.)

Keep along the high ground until you can see a way down to the narrow strip of land which links Cromor with Eilean Orasaidh (pronounced Orosay and meaning 'ebb tide island'). The crossing may not be possible during an exceptionally high tide, but normally it is a few steps on dry but seaweed encrusted rocks to a gap in the wall at the other side. Cross the

Loch nam Bodach.

Looking towards Eilean Orasaidh.

broken fence and go left to a ruined shelter round the corner. From this point the whole of this small island is yours to explore. Some areas support a growth of strong heather which makes walking difficult, but it is quite easy to pick a way to the high point at 53m from where the views are extremely fine. Drop down to the east side and make your way back to the crossing place on the south of the island.

Cross over the gap and go up the grassy slope ahead, turning left (south) along the west side of the high ground. The next point to aim for is the tidal outlet from Loch nam Bodach (loch of the old man) which lies below you on the right. This outlet is hidden from view until you are almost there, but is found after passing a small island and drawing level with a long promontory on the other side of the loch.

Take care crossing the stepping stones here. This point may be impassable at high tide, in which event you should be prepared to circumnavigate Loch nam Bodach. If you cross the stepping stones, go past the end of the loch and pick up an old path which contours above some old lazy-beds and passes a standing stone. When a croft is reached, follow the lane into Cromor. Turn left at a T-junction and then right to complete the circuit.

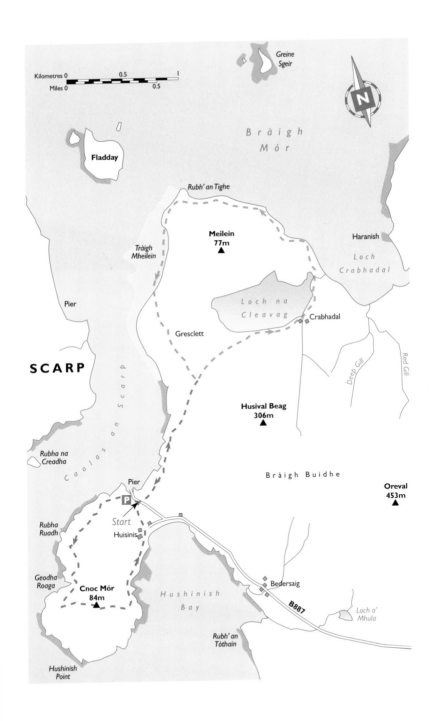

# HUISINIS (HUSHINISH)

The Huisinis peninsula is the most westerly point of the Harris hills and faces the Island of Scarp across a narrow sound, Caolas an Scarp. At the time of writing, Scarp is deserted, although not long ago there were as many as 50 inhabitants and the island had its own school. There is a fine sandy beach at Huisinis and an even finer one at Meilein which is backed by high dunes.

Huisinis is approached by a long single-track road which branches off the A859 3 km/2 miles north of Tarbert. It passes the old whaling station of Bunavoneadar, (foot of the place between the rivers) where there is a prominent chimney stack, and later goes through the private grounds of Abhainn Suidhe (pronounced Avunsoo-i, river of the seat). This Victorian castle was built in 1868 and belongs to the North Harris Estate. The grounds are attractive, with a series of small waterfalls cascading into the sea from Loch Leosaid.

Huisinis is within the North Harris SSSI, which covers a large area between Loch Resort and West Loch Tarbert and between the west coast and Glen Langadale in the east. The area is of particular interest to biologists as a fine example of an ecosystem resulting from strong oceanic conditions. Vegetation is typical of acid peat uplands overlying Lewisian gneiss and granite, with species-poor wet heath. Many features are intermediate between those found on St Kilda and those on the mainland Lewisian and Moine hills.

This walk explores the area in two directions from the same point, so it is easy to shorten the walk by only tackling one of the circular routes. The small peninsula to the south-west is particularly good for seabirds. Gannets, terns and cormorants may be seen and fulmars nest on a north-facing cliff at Geodha Roaga. If you are lucky you may see black-throated divers.

## INFORMATION

**Distance:** 11 km (7 miles) with 265 m of ascent.

**Map:** OS Landranger sheet 13, West Lewis and North Harris.

**Start and finish:** The pier at North Hushinish. From Tarbert take the Stornoway road and turn left after about 3 km onto B887. At Hushinish turn right onto a sandy track 100 m before the houses and park on the road verge near the pier.

**Terrain:** Mainly easy walking on grass and a well-made path, but the descent to Loch na Clavaig can be very boggy. Boots are advisable.

**Time:** 3–4 hours.

**Note:** North Harris Estates should be contacted before doing this walk during the stalking season (July to October).

Sound of Scarp at Tràigh Mheilein.

Walking to the north-east gives a longer route, which takes you to the remote croft of Crabhadal, no longer a full-time croft but still in occasional use. The changing sea colours as the tide advances and recedes over the sand in the shallow waters of the Sound are particularly attractive.

To make the circuit of the Huisinis peninsula, follow the coast round on the north side, crossing a fence by a stile. Keep above the low cliffs and then descend to a small lochan. A sheep-track which is almost a path zig-zags up at the side of the cliffs above Geodha Roaga, where in springtime birds nest among the ledges. Contour around the hill for a short way and then turn east and make for the little top of Cnoc Mor (84 m). Descend east towards the coast and return on the grass at the edge of the land to a gate just before the houses. A track leads across the machair to the pier (3.5 km or 2 miles).

To begin the second and longer circuit, go to the right and through a gate, following the path to a stile. The path, which can be seen from the start of the walk, hugs the steep cliffs of Husival Beag above on the right. Rising fairly high to avoid two small ravines, it leads to a low pass south of Gresclett.

Loch na Cleavag.

Birds to look out for include golden plover, wheatear, stonechat, wren, meadow and rock pipits and ravens. But this is golden eagle country, so keep on looking upwards. These beautiful birds like to nest on remote crags, in which this area abounds, and there is no finer sight than one of these splendid creatures gliding effortlessly along as it quarters the ground in search of prey (usually rabbits and hares).

Proceed to Loch na Cleavag and past Crabhadal and then along the edge of the loch to the headland of Meilein (Rubh' an Tighe). There is a fine view into the narrow fjord of Loch Resort, which is the boundary between Harris and Lewis. Cross some lazybeds and continue over the headland to reach the sands of Meilein beach. To return, follow the upward track, climbing up the side of Gresclett, and rejoin the path used on the outward route.

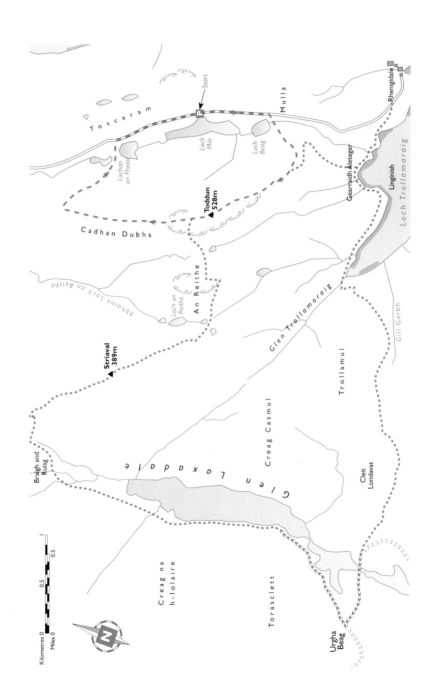

# TODDUN

Toddun, an attractive mountain of 528 m, lies west of Loch Siophort (Seaforth), a long arm of the sea that stretches inland for 22 km and separates North Harris from the Pairc (Park) area of Lewis. The name means simply 'sea fjord'. When approaching Tarbert on the ferry from Skye, Toddun stands out as an attractive sugarloaf shape in the end-on view of its summit ridge. It is equally impressive when seen from the north, travelling along the main

Toddun—view from summit ridge.

road from Stornoway to Tarbert. On a good day there are outstanding and panoramic views including St Kilda to the west and An Teallach, Slioch and Liathach on the mainland, with Skye looking only a short distance away.

## INFORMATION

**Distance:** 6 km (4 miles) with 360 m of ascent.

**Map:** OS Landranger sheet 14, Tarbert and Loch Seaforth.

**Start and finish:** At GR 217036 on the new road from Maaruig to Rhenigidale, on the east side of Loch Mor. From Tarbert, drive towards Stornoway and turn right after 13 km/8 miles (note that this road is not shown on most maps).

**Terrain:** Pathless but easy walking on a well-defined ridge, on grassy trods and bare rock. Boots advisable.

**Time:** About 2½ hours.

Toddun from Scalpay.

This short walk starts at a high point and gives a rewarding mountaineering experience without undue effort. Those who would like a more demanding excursion can make a longer circuit by including Straiaval, Glen Laxadale and the good path that leads from Urgha Beag to Reinigeadal (Rhenigidale). For strong walkers staying at the Gatliff Trust hostel in Rhenigidale, this is an obvious choice.

The vegetation in this area is of particular interest to botanists and includes different types of heathland with a variety of mosses and liverworts. A rare moss, *Bazzania pearsonii*, grows among the heather on the middle slopes. On the north-eastern slopes the heath is locally rich in Atlantic liverworts, seven different species being recorded. On the summit ridge there are deep and dense carpets of moss, while the south-western slopes of the hill support a mixture of dense heathers, among which are several liverworts.

Walk along the road towards Rhenigidale to the far end of the circular Loch Beag. Cross the outlet near a sheep fank and make a rising traverse to meet the south-east ridge of Toddun on easy ground with useful sheep tracks. Continue up the ridge, which gives delightful walking, often with a choice of ways on grass or easy rocks. The ridge is defined by steep ground on both sides and is narrow enough to give a sense of airiness without any cause for alarm.

At the top, follow the ridge down in an almost northerly direction at first. Continue until well past the steep ground on the right-hand side and then strike back in a south-easterly direction on easy ground to cross the valley between two small lochans. There may be temporary fences to negotiate, erected to protect reseeded ground.

Toddun from the north.

Try to walk round the fenced areas if possible, but if you have to cross a fence, then do so carefully. Walk along the road to return to your car.

To climb Toddun from Rhenigidale, leave the new road along the path heading west above Loch Trollamaraig and follow it as far as Gearraidh Aleteger. Strike on up the south-eastern slopes to gain the ridge and continue to the summit. Start going down the north ridge until you can see a way of descending the western slopes which avoids steep rock, and head over An Reithe before making for the top of Straiaval (389 m).

A careful descent north-west is made to reach the bealach on the old grass-covered road which leads from Maaruig to the mouth of Glen Laxadale (glen of salmon). With the return to Rhenigidale over the north shoulder of Beinn a'Chaolais this route involves a walk of at least 18 km, much of it over pathless ground. It is only recommended for experienced hillwalkers who are used to route-finding.

Glen Laxadale from Kyles road.

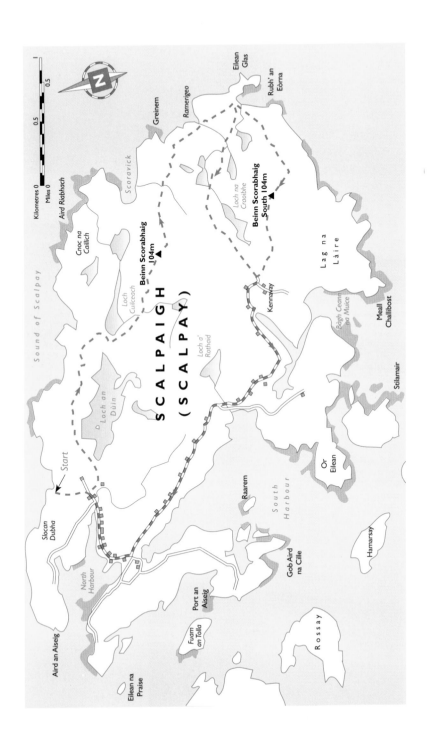

# SCALPAIGH

Scalpaigh (Scalpay) is a prosperous island with many new and restored houses. The economy is based on fishing, thanks to the excellent sheltered anchorages. The thriving community of about 500 has a shop, a school and at the time of writing the frequent ferry service is due to be replaced by a bridge. At the far eastern end of the island is the lighthouse of Eilean Glas, one of the first four built in Scotland in 1788. At one time it was the only lighthouse in the Western Isles. The light is now automatic and the buildings have been converted into holiday accommodation: a delightfully remote place, but you have to carry your supplies in across a moorland path.

This circular walk over the highest point of the island, Beinn Scorabhaig (Ben Scoravick) at 104 m, is an intriguing route which threads its way over moorland and between lochs, then descends to the east coast and

Scalpay lighthouse.

on to the lighthouse. There is a choice of two waymarked routes from the lighthouse over the moor to the road end. The views to the North Harris hills from Ben Scoravick are very fine. To the east, the high mountains of Torridon can be seen on a good day, with the Shiant Islands in the foreground and Skye to the south.

An option for anyone preferring a shorter walk is to take a car over on the ferry and drive on to Ceann a

## INFORMATION

**Distance:** 12 km (7½ miles) and 230 m of ascent.

**Map:** OS Landranger sheet 14, Tarbert and Loch Seaforth, or Pathfinder sheet 108, Scalpay.

**Start and finish:** The ferry pier on Scalpay. From Tarbert drive east to Caolas Scalpaigh (Kyles of Scalpay). There are frequent car ferries, e.g. 0915, 1015, 1115, return 1500, 1615, 1720 (no Sunday service). Check ferry times locally.

**Terrain:** Pathless and boggy in places. Easy return along a country road. Boots advisable.

**Time:** 3½–4 hours.

**Refreshments:** At the lighthouse (summer only).

**Toilets:** At the ferry terminal at Kyles of Scalpay.

Bhaigh (Kennavay), then make a circular walk to the lighthouse by means of the two waymarked paths.

Walk up the road from the ferry and at a T-junction turn left towards a new bungalow, then right along a track which swings left to Loch an Duin. Just before reaching the loch, cross the burn near a fence and go through a gate. Follow sheep tracks by the fence and then over several rocky heather-covered knolls which border the north side of the loch. After going through a gate in a cross fence the ground becomes grassy and gives pleasant walking. Continue along the high ground, making a short diversion left to view an attractive and hidden lochan in a deep hollow surrounded by steep crags. Return to the narrow track leading over a low col and down to another loch, Loch Cuilceach. A large cairn by some peat banks makes a good landmark from which several convenient sheep tracks head in the direction of Beinn Scorabhaig and provide easy walking. The top is in sight most of the way.

Before reaching the top, there is some fun to be had threading a way through a maze of peat hags, relieved by slabby outcrops of grey gneiss. There are two tops,

North harbour, Scalpay.

separated by a dry peat area. After enjoying the view and picking out distant features on the mainland, start descending eastwards at first, heading roughly towards the Shiant Islands and some bright green grass near the coast. Gradually turn south-east, keeping above the low crags where several sheep tracks avoid the wet areas. The prominent wall across the end of the peninsula is easily surmounted where it abuts against the rock at the small inlet of Ramerigeo. Go up the hill ahead to pick up a well-built track leading to the lighthouse. Two of the buildings are at the time of writing occupied all the year round and you may meet some of the 12 feline residents, some of whom walk with their owner as far as the small harbour.

To return, follow the path inland to a gate in the high wall at the edge of a lochan and follow the yellow posts which mark the way across the moor to a fenced electric substation. From this a motorable track leads to Kennavay. Go through an open gate and down a steep hill to another gate which is kept closed. Turn right and follow the road back to the ferry. A slightly longer return route to Kennavay which is rather more attractive and also less boggy is a path with red markers, leading south-west at first to another gate in the high wall. This path swings left, then right and more or less follows the telegraph poles, reaching the road by the open gate at the top of the steep hill.

Although the final part of the walk is along a surfaced road, there is little traffic to disturb the walker and some lovely views along the way, including a narrow sea loch and the South and North harbours.

Sound of Scalpay.

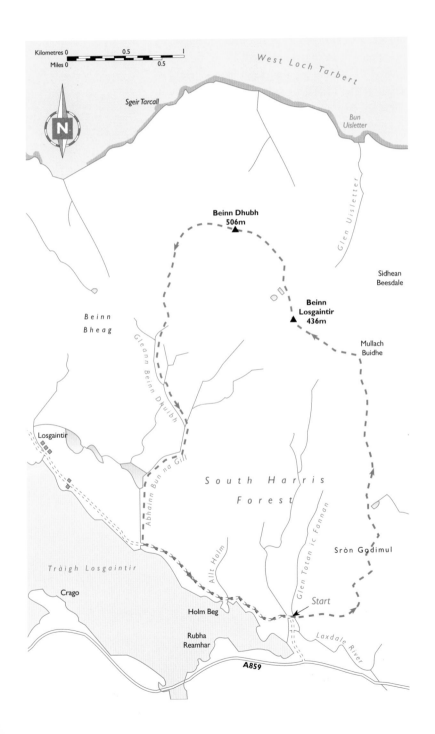

# BEINN LOSGAINTIR AND BEINN DHUBH

## INFORMATION

**Distance:** 10 km (6 miles) and 556 m of ascent.

**Map:** OS Landranger sheet 14, Tarbert and Loch Seaforth.

**Start and finish:** From the A859 Tairbeart to An t-Ob (Tarbert-Leverburgh) road take the narrow road on the right towards Losgaintir, 12 km after leaving Tarbert. Park on the left in 1 km, shortly after a sharp left-hand bend at GR 094974.

**Terrain:** Mainly pathless but all easy ground.

**Time:** About 4 hours.

The Losgaintir (Luskentyre) hills lie between Loch a Siar (West Loch Tarbert) and the beautiful and extensive Luskentyre sands (Traigh Losgaintir), the views of which from the ascent route are outstanding. The summit of Beinn Dhubh at 506 m is the highest point on the ridge, and from here the hills of North Harris are seen to perfection. For full enjoyment of this walk, it is well worth waiting for a good day.

From the parking place, walk back over the bridge and go left through a gate onto the open moorland. Make a rising traverse eastwards towards the long southerly spur of Sron Godimul, which is then followed upwards. Rock slabs at a gentle angle give pleasant, easy walking.

On a good day, rest stops will be frequent for the full appreciation of the view opening up below. The changing colours of the waters of Traigh Losgaintir are irresistible to photographers, with violets, blues and greens giving way to soft pearly greys between gold and silver sands as the tide recedes. The channel of Faodhail Losgaintir is a serpentine curve of deep aquamarine winding through the gradually drying sands.

This area is not only very beautiful but also of great scientific interest, particularly for coastal

Looking across Luskentyre Bay to Toe Head.

geomorphology, and is listed as an SSSI. Luskentyre Banks include some of the highest sand hills in the Outer Hebrides, with both erosional and depositional features, and the dynamic spit of Corran Seilebost opposite the Banks includes machair and dune landforms. The whole complex, including the intertidal sand beach of Traigh Losgaintir and the adjacent saltmarsh, is of great significance for the study of coastal evolution.

At the top of Sron Godimul the ground flattens out. Walk past a small lochan and then a cairn on a boulder marking the spot height of 287 m. Continue climbing steadily up the broad and grassy ridge to Mullach Buidhe (yellow hill) where the main ridge curving round from Ceann Reamhar is met and the hills to the north can be seen across Loch a Siar (West Loch Tarbert).

The low-growing vegetation on the flanks and on the summit ridge is a joy to walk on. Botanists may be interested to know that it includes a good selection of mosses and liverworts. The north-east slopes of the area in particular have a liverwort-rich heath of international importance.

Follow the ridge north-west to the top of Beinn Losgaintir (436 m) on which is a large white cairn.

Toe Head from Ben Luskentyre.

From here the short descent to a lochan on a broad col and the final ascent to the east top of Beinn Dhubh (black hill) takes about half an hour. The long flat top runs east-west with the 506 m trig point surrounded by a shelter wall in the centre.

Walk down the west ridge to a prominent knoll with several large cairns, another superb viewpoint. Continue down grassy slopes towards Losgaintir (approximately south-west) until the ground becomes distinctly steeper. At this point bear left and make for the corner of a fence by a small burn in the flat valley of Gleann Beinn Dhuibh. Walk down the side of the burn on good ground and into a miniature ravine with ferns growing on a shady wall.

When the burn makes a right-angled bend, go down the right bank near a fence to reach a dam where the water is diverted to some lochans above the village. Turn left and follow the fence down to the road, where a low fence is easily stepped over. Walk back along the road, or along the sand if the tide is out. Go quietly here and if you are very lucky you might just see an otter among the rocks, as the author once did, making a superb ending to a most enjoyable walk.

View across West Loch Tarbert from Ben Luskentyre.

A longer round can be made of all the Losgaintir tops by starting up the rugged Uaval Mor (358 m) in the south-east and continuing over Ceann Reamhar (467 m). A descent is made to a bealach overlooking the impressively steep north-facing corrie of Beesdale before rising up to Mullach Buidhe and joining the route described.

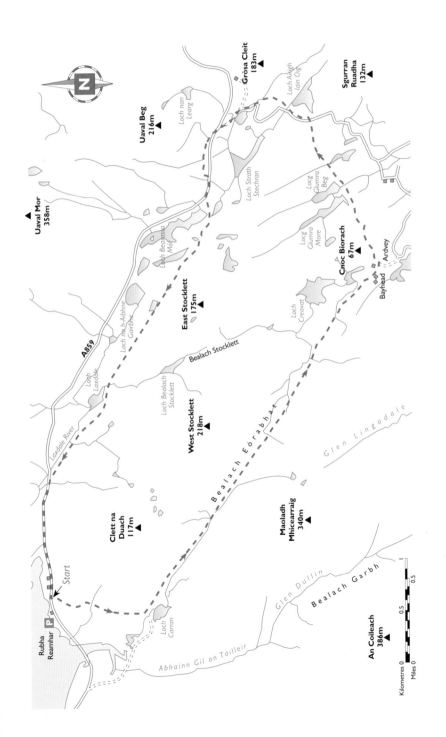

Gròsa Cleit
183m

Sgurran
Ruadha
132m

Uaval Beg
216m

Loch nan
Learg

Loch Airigh
Iain Oig

Uaval Mor
358m

Loch Strath
Stechran

Locg
Glumra
Beg

Loch Beannsa
Mór

Locg
Glumra
More

Cnoc Biorach
67m

Ardvey

East Stocklett
175m

Bayhead

Loch na h-Aibhne
Gairbhe

A859

Bealach Stocklett

Loch
Creavat

Loch
Laxdale

Loch Bealach
Stocklett

West Stocklett
218m

Bealach Eòrabhat

Glen Lingadale

Laxdale River

Clett na
Duach
117m

Maoladh
Mhicearraig
340m

Start

Glen Dullin

Bealach Garbh

Rubha
Reamhar

Loch
Carran

An Coileach
386m

Abhainn Gil an Tàilleir

Kilometres 0   0.5
Miles 0   0.5

# SEILEBOST TO BAYHEAD

This circular walk makes use of an old road which was originally used to carry coffins from the east coast for burial on the west, there being insufficient depth of soil on the east. Place names in the old graveyard at Losgaintir include Stocinis, Geocrab, Plocropol and so on. The large cairns you will notice on this route, especially near the summit of the pass, were erected by the funeral parties when they stopped to rest.

The walk clearly shows the contrast between the Bays area in the east and the machairs of the west coast. The Bays is unique with its highly indented coastline, bare rocky landscape and many lochans. Originally settled by the Vikings as shown by the placenames of Norse origin, it has never been able to support a large population owing to its unsuitablity for agriculture (see Walk 11 for more about this area).

The machairs of the west, with wide sandy bays and a wealth of wild flowers on the lime-enriched land, present a completely different picture. The land is capable of cultivation and has been inhabited from earliest times. In the 19th century the crofters were evicted to make way for sheep, and the present settlements date only from the 1920s. The scenic beauty of the area helps modern crofters to supplement their income from sheep and fishing by providing accommodation for visitors.

## INFORMATION

**Distance:** 13½ km/8½ miles with 245 m of ascent.

**Map:** OS Landranger sheet 14, Tarbert and Loch Seaforth.

**Start and finish:** A small carpark at NGR GR089971, between the Losgaintir (Luskentyre) road junction and Seilebost. Approaching from Tarbert on A859, this is on the right hand side about 500 m past the junction.

**Terrain:** Mainly easy walking on good tracks and paths, apart from a boggy section near the Bealach Eòrabhat. Near Bayhead the path has been improved and waymarked by green and yellow posts. Boots advisable.

**Time:** About 4½–5 hours.

Luskentyre Bay.

Traigh Losgaintir (Luskentyre Bay) is a Site of Special Scientific Interest (SSSI) and has been partly described in walk 9. One area of interest is the birdlife, which includes the now rare and elusive corncrake. It is often heard calling in a harsh and rasping tone, but is notoriously difficult to observe. Midsummer is the most likely time, but you will be lucky even then to catch a glimpse of one skulking among the vegetation.

This walk could, if preferred, be started at Bayhead, in which case it is best done in a clockwise direction. The advantage then is that the lovely view over Luskentyre Bay and out to the island of Tarasaigh (Taransay) gradually opens up on the descent from the Bealach Eorabhat.

For those who would like a short walk, a circuit can be made by turning right at the junction near Loch Carran and returning along the road from Seilebost. The slight height gain opens up the view considerably.

From the car park, go back towards Tarbert for a few metres to find the start of the walk. The start of the track is signposted. From here it is excellent walking to a junction near Loch Carran, which has been dammed. After going over a stile at this junction, turn left and go up the grassy track which leads south-east in a long gradual ascent over the Bealach Eorabhat. This pass is also known as Bealach Creig an Eoin (pass of the crag of the birds) because of the steep cliffs on the lower slopes of Maoladh Mhicearraig, a 340m hill on the south-west of the pass.

After passing a small loch, the track dwindles to a path and finally becomes a meandering route through the bog. The waymark posts begin here. As Loch Creavat is reached, the path has been restored and improved by drainage and causeways over the wet parts.

When the house at Ceann a Bhaigh (Bayhead) is reached, turn left to cross a footbridge and go over a stile. Waymarks are particularly helpful here as the path rises in zigzags and is not obvious. The way then continues outside a fenced area. This section is

delightful walking on a well constructed and dry path, passing south of Lochs Glumra Mor and Beag before reaching a narrow unfenced road. Turn left, and after crossing a bridge find the continuation of the old path (on the right) which bypasses a bend in the road.

Above Bayhead.

Before the road joins the A859 at a T-junction, turn left along a section of old road. Walk a short distance on the new main road until the old road can be picked up again on the right. After rejoining the new road, look out for the old road once again on the left after about 200 m. Stay on this road now as it leads through a quarry, unfortunately used as a rubbish dump. The dumps include an amazing collection of defunct trucks, diggers and other machinery which almost qualifies for museum status.

The track rises slightly over a shoulder, then descends past Loch Laxdale and an inhabited house before rejoining the road. Turn left and walk along the road for 1 km to return to the starting point, with the views of Traigh Losgaintir opening out before you as you walk. This is a particularly beautiful sight in the evening.

Seilebost from Luskentyre. The Bayhead track leads through U-shaped gap right of centre.

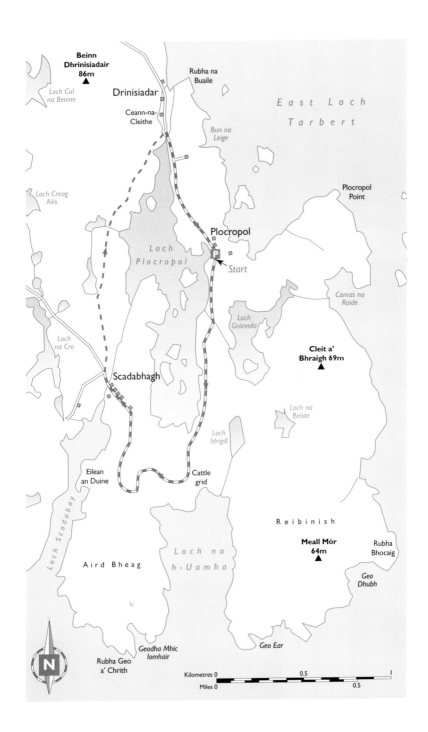

# PLOCROPOL

The Bays of the east coast of Harris are a unique and interesting area where the bare bedrock of Lewisian gneiss is exposed over much of the surface. There are a myriad lochs and lochans, shallow peat beds and a very thin layer of soil supporting a low growth of heather. It was and still is an inhospitable place to live. At one time the area was almost uninhabited, except when people from the machair villages on the west side came over in the summer, bringing cattle to graze and to do some fishing.

For a short time income was obtained from the kelp industry, but the collapse of this, combined with an influx of people forced to leave the machair by the inhumane acts of the landowners in clearing the western areas for sheep, led to a situation where the Bays area was severely overpopulated. Without any good land, the people resorted to the creation of so-called 'lazybeds', where the little soil available was piled up into strips and enriched with seaweed and manure, and on which potatoes were grown.

Today the fish farming industry is bringing some new employment to the area, and the Harris Tweed industry, encouraged and developed by Lady Dunmore, one-time owner of Harris, is still flourishing,

## INFORMATION

**Distance:** 5 km (3 miles).

**Map:** OS Landranger sheet 14, Tarbert and Loch Seaforth, or OS Pathfinder sheet 108, Scalpay (Harris).

**Start and finish:** Parking area in Plocropol at GR 179935. From Tarbert take the road towards Leverburgh and go left at the 2nd turn, signposted Plocrapool/ Plocropol 3.

**Terrain:** Easy walking on a quiet road and a good path. No special footwear needed.

**Time:** About 1½ hours.

Plocropol under a stormy sky.

although there is an ageing population and many houses remain empty. Harris Tweed is mostly made from the wool of the blackfaced sheep which are sheared early in summer. Originally the wool was cleaned and dyed in the small croft houses using dyestuffs from local plants, a favourite being crotal, a grey lichen scraped from the rocks which produces a rich brown colour. After further washing and drying, the wool was prepared for spinning and weaving.

Now much of the dyeing, spinning and finishing takes place in mills, but the cloth is still produced by individual craftworkers, each with his or her own loom. 'Harris Tweed' can be produced anywhere in the Outer Hebrides but must be handwoven and made from 100% pure new wool in order to qualify for the Orb trademark of the Harris Tweed Association. There are some 450 independent weavers, and some of them give demonstrations, including one in Plocropol.

At the present time, major changes are afoot with moves to introduce new looms producing double width cloth, for which there is a greater demand. Several crofts in this area sell cloth, knitting wools and knitwear.

Lazybeds near Plocropol.

Scenically the area has great attractions, with many rocky bays and inlets and tiny islands. Among the brown of the heather moorland are bright green patches where sheep graze. On sunny days the lochans are a brilliant blue, bedecked with water lilies in summer, and yellow flags bloom near the old lazybeds. Stands of small trees are seen on islands in the lochs, mainly willow and rowan with sometimes honeysuckle, out of reach of the sheep. This walk from Plocropol is typical of the area.

Walk south on the narrow surfaced road along the side of Loch Plocropol, a pretty loch with several small islands. The road becomes unfenced and there are pleasant viewpoints over the loch. Look out on the left for an island in Loch Grannda, densely covered with trees. As the cattle grid is reached, make a short diversion left to look at Loch na h-Uamha (loch of caves), an attractive bay with rocky cliffs either side.

Continue along the road, which winds through the scattered houses of Scadabhagh (Scadabay), until an old chapel is seen on the right. Turn right through a gate and pass to the left of the chapel, picking up an excellent track which leads north to reach the tarmac road at the head of Loch Plocropol. This is a well-made track, built up over the boggy stretches, because it was once the original road before the present road was built. Several gates cross this track, and if you find them closed, please ensure you re-close them behind you. There are fine views of the hills to the north.

Author with orphan lamb.

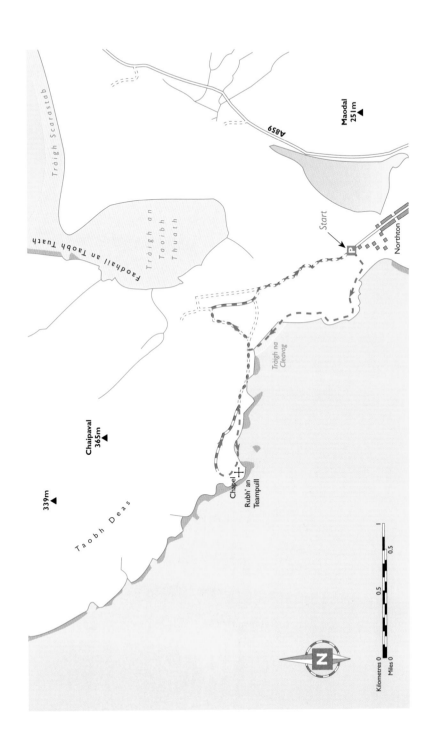

Maodal
251m ▲

Tràigh Scarastab

Tràigh an
Taoibh
Thuath

Faodhail an Taobh Tuath

Start

Northton

Tràigh na
Cleavag

Chaipaval
365m ▲

339m ▲

Taobh Deas

Chapel
Rubh' an
Teampuill

A859

Kilometres 0
Miles 0

0.5
0.5

1

N

# TOE HEAD CHAPEL

Toe Head is a peninsula which is almost an island, separated from the rest of Harris by the flat expanse of the golden Scarista sands (Tràigh Sgarasta) and a low-lying marsh area near Northton (Taobh Tuath in Gaelic). The area of Northton has been inhabited for a long period of time, an archaeological excavation in 1966 showing evidence of habitation from about 3000BC onwards. Fragments of pottery known as Beakerware (because of the shape of the complete pots) were found. In the midden site outside the house were found large quantities of emptied sea-shells, as well as the bones of sheep, cattle, deer and birds, giving evidence of a varied diet.

**INFORMATION**

**Distance:** 6 km (4 miles).

**Map:** OS Landranger sheet 18, Sound of Harris.

**Start and finish:** Northton road end. From Tarbert drive south along A859 towards Leverburgh and in 27 km (4 km after passing Scarista), turn sharp right into Northton. Go through the gate at the road end and park on the grass. Do not drive on the machair as it is very fragile.

**Terrain:** Easy walking all the way on turf or sand. No special footwear needed.

**Time:** 2 hours, but worth spending longer here on a good day.

Approaching ruined chapel, Toe Head.

This walk to the ruined chapel on Rubh' an Teampuill is a delightful short excursion with superb views across the Sound of Harris to Pabbay and the Uists. The chapel is believed to have been built in the 16th century at about the same time as St Clement's church at Rodel, which is also well worth a visit. Toe Head (Gob an Tobha) itself has a number of natural arches and can be reached in a longer, more strenuous walk by following the coastline on the east and north sides. The summit of the peninsula, Chaipaval, is a shapely hill of 365 m and is seen to advantage at the start of this walk.

This route goes through part of the Northton Bay Site of Special Scientific Interest (SSSI); a site which

Wild flowers on the ruined chapel wall.

covers over 1000 acres and is of interest for its botany, ornithology and geology. It includes a variety of habitats which show a transition from calcareous areas to acid moorland. From the large area of shell sand at Sgarasta there is a gradation to saltmarsh, brackish water fen, sand dunes and machair, with a coastal lagoon near Northton.

One of the most striking features of the area is a band of rock known as the Chaipaval pegmatite. This band is 25 m thick in places and over 1.5 km long, so it is easily seen from anywhere in the area as a prominent and continuous dyke-like structure standing out pale among the dark heather on the lower slopes of Chaipaval.

The rock has been quarried for potash feldspar and is well-exposed in two large excavations at the north-east end, where interesting specimens may be found in the spoil heaps. Some 16 different minerals have been recorded, one of them, betafite, unknown elsewhere in Britain. Masses of pure muscovite can be found *in situ* at the base of one of the opencast workings. Anyone interested in geology will find explorations in this area very rewarding.

To start the walk, turn left and cross the grass to a stile which gives access to Tràigh an Taoibh Thuath (Northton beach). Stay on the landward side of the fence and follow it round the low headland, where there are usually fulmars. Cross the beach ahead, Traigh na Cleavag, then go up to join the pleasant grassy path which leads to the ruined chapel. Pass the second beach and then cross a third beach to reach the headland and the ruins of the chapel. The walls stand high but there is no roof. Wild flowers such as thrift and patches of yellow lichen grow on the walls.

Return by the grassy inland path and when the large beach is reached, bear left on a track which leads to a marvellous viewpoint across sand and sea to the Harris hills. When another track is joined, turn right to return to the start. This area of machair at the edge of the marsh is excellent for birds, in fact it is the best place in Lewis and Harris for breeding waders and a feeding area for wildfowl. Species recorded as breeding include greylag geese, shelduck, teal, oystercatchers, dunlin, snipe, lapwings, redshanks, ringed plovers, wheatears and many more.

Keen hill walkers who wish to reach the top of Chaipaval can do so by the steep heathery slopes above the chapel, but a more rewarding way is to make an anti-clockwise approach to Toe Head. Follow the coastline closely, passing at first signs of earlier cultivation and later on looking down some spectacular gullies. The author once had a close view of a young golden eagle feeding on a carcase in one of these gullies. Disturbed by our presence, the only way it could take off was to pass close to us in the confines of the rock walls, a truly memorable sight.

Chaipaval.

On reaching the end of the peninsula where there are several natural rock arches, follow the ridge roughly south-east to a subsidiary top at 339 m, and then walk across a dip to the main top at 365 m. On a good day the views include St.Kilda, 65 km to the west, and the Cuillins of Skye, 75 km to the southeast, with spectacular views of the tidal currents in the Sound of Harris. For the descent, it is best to head north-east for some distance to avoid steep ground before turning south and making for the track back across the machair.

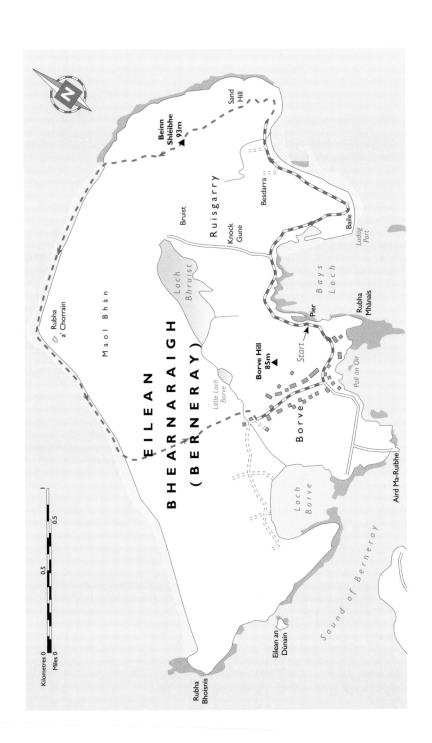

# EILEAN BHEARNARAIGH (BERNERAY)

The island of Bearnaraigh (Berneray) measures only 6 km by 2.5 km and lies in the Sound of Harris close to the northern tip of North Uist, from which it is most easily reached by a passenger boat from Newtonferry. There is a car ferry to the south-east of the island, where most of the population of about 150 live. The construction of the car ferry and three new township roads has done much to help reverse the decline in population, which stood at over 500 in 1901. Today it is a thriving community of crofters and fishermen.

The island can also be reached by a passenger ferry from An t-Ob (Leverburgh). The north end of the island is particularly attractive and there are outstanding views from the highest point, Beinn Shleibhe. (I was told by a resident that this is known locally as Beinn Lever.)

The mountains of South Harris are close by to the north-east, the Uists to the south and across the Little Minch lies Skye with every detail visible on a clear day. This circular walk is a particularly varied one with a grassy hill, a long deserted beach and a crossing of the low grassy machair of the interior.

From the pier, go up to the coast road and turn right. Follow this narrow lane around Bays Loch, ignoring a

## INFORMATION

**Distance:** 13 km (8 miles), with 125 m of ascent.

**Map:** OS Landranger sheet 18, Sound of Harris.

**Start and finish:** Berneray pier. From North Uist there are ferries at 0900 or 1130, return 1730. No ferry on Sundays. A new Sound of Harris ferry is due to start in 1996.

**Terrain:** All easy walking on roads, tracks, grass and sand. No special footwear needed, but boots advisable in wet weather.

**Time:** 3½–4 hours.

**Refreshments:** The Community Centre in Borve, seen on the right as you come into the township, serves refreshments in summer but is closed Sunday and Monday.

Gatliff Hostel, Berneray.

left turn and going out to the point where the Gatliff Trust use two thatched houses as a hostel (it is open all the year round and sleeps 9). Turn north and walk along the lane which leads to Sand Hill farm. On the way the ruins of a church are seen across the fields. This church was built in 1827 to a standard design by the noted civil engineer Thomas Telford, better known, perhaps for his work on roads, bridges and the Caledonian Canal. This design was one of several used for churches all over the Highlands and Islands. Pass behind the ruined farm and below the new bungalow above, following the grassy track through a pair of gateposts and on to a ruined house. Please keep to the path here, as this is private ground.

Toe Head from Beinn Shleibhe.

From the ruins, start walking up the gentle slopes of Beinn Ghainche (Sand Hill) on close-cropped turf. All the way up there are fine views across the Sound of Harris to enjoy. At the top, aim for the gap in the fence ahead where there is a fallen gate and continue up easy ground to the top of Beinn Shleibhe (93 m). After enjoying the views in all directions, drop down, heading north-west to the coast, keeping to the right of a fence and gaining access to the beach at the point where the dunes abut against rocks. The island of Pabaigh (Pabbay) seen across the sound is uninhabited but supports a small herd of deer.

Walk along the firm sand, which you are most likely to have to yourself, for almost 2 km to Rubh' a' Chorrain where the corner is turned and the long west beach of Bearnaraigh lies before you. This beach is backed by a magnificent chain of high sand dunes which shelter the interior of the island, low lying machair where cattle graze.

Beach and dunes, North Berneray.

To complete the circle walk along the beach for about 1.5 km (1 mile). There are no landmarks so it is difficult to be precise about this. It is also unnecessary as it is easy to find a convenient gap in the sandhills and go up to get your bearings. The township of Borve is the place to make for, aiming for the left hand corner of the enclosing fence.

Before continuing you might like to make a short diversion to try to identify the two 'chairstones' among a group of boulders, said to be used for the settling of disputes. Follow the fence round to an open gate which gives access to the road at the bottom of a hill. Pass the community centre and follow the road back to the ferry, which takes about 25 minutes.

If you are staying overnight, you could extend this walk to make a complete circuit of the island. To do this, continue walking along the west beach where you can look across to the island of Boreray. When the low cliffs begin, a grassy track leads through the sand dunes and across the machair, passing below a ruined hut on Cnoc nan Claigean (eerily named Hill of Skulls, because the skulls of victims executed at the chairstones are said to be buried here).

Turn left through a gate and either follow the firm track leading to the Community Centre at Borve, or follow the coast, passing the commemorative cairn to Aonghas MacAskill, the giant of Berneray. Continue past the burial ground towards Loch Borve, a tidal loch which is all sand at low tide. A track leads over a stone bridge and joins the route to Borve.

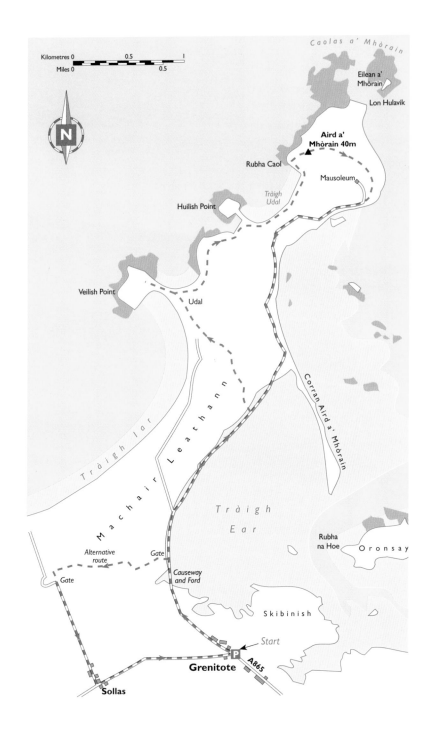

Kilometres 0    0.5    1
Miles 0    0.5

N

Caolas a' Mhòrain

Eilean a'
Mhòrain

Lon Hulavik

Aird a'
Mhòrain 40m

Rubha Caol

Mausoleum

Tràigh
Udal

Huilish Point

Veilish Point

Udal

Corran Aird a' Mhòrain

Tràigh Iar

Machair Leathann

Tràigh
Ear

Rubha
na Hoe    Oronsay

Alternative
route    Gate

Gate    Causeway
and Ford

Skibinish

Start

P

Gate

A865

Grenitote

Sollas

# THE GRENITOTE HEADLAND

This narrow finger of land projecting northwards from North Uist is an attractive stretch of machair between sandy beaches. On the west side are two small headlands, Veilish Point and Huilish Point, and on the east is a narrow sand bar covered with marram grass and sheltering the extensive sandy bay, Traigh Iar. At Aird a' Mhòrain there is a high dune system rising to 40 m from where there are magnificent views. On a clear day St Kilda

can be seen about 70 km away to the west. To the north-east the Toe Head peninsula and the hills of South Harris stand out beyond Boreray, Berneray and Pabbay.

On the way to Aird a' Mhòrain, the route traverses the Machair Leathann, one of the places where the machair of the Western Isles is seen at its best. The underlying soil has been greatly enriched by shell-blown sand and in summer offers a magnificent display of wild flowers. These include primroses and pansies in early May, then cranesbill, corn marigold, vipers bugloss and many other species. The machair is invaluable to the crofters who have enclosed many acres to grow crops of oats and rye to use as animal fodder. It is essential that walkers take great care never to walk on growing crops, keeping to field edges whenever necessary.

## INFORMATION

**Distance:** 13 km (8 miles).

**Map:** OS Landranger sheet 18, Sound of Harris.

**Start and finish:** The telephone box by the road junction at Grenitote on the A865, 14 km north-west from Lochmaddy.

**Terrain:** Easy walking on sand, paths and tracks. No special footwear needed.

**Time:** Allow 3½–4 hours.

Sands at Grenitote.

Many birds nest among the cereal crops including a colony of arctic terns and a few little terns, which are a protected species. Fulmars nest on the ground too and so do dunlin, ringed plover and snipe, all of which should be left undisturbed. From the headlands eider, shelduck and occasionally divers may be seen.

At Udal there is an archaeological site still being excavated and believed to have been occupied from the Neolithic Age to the late 17th century, when a

Traigh Udal.

Dunes at Balranald SW of Grenitote.

sandstorm completely engulfed the village in 1697. Please observe it from the outside of the fenced area, so as to protect the site.

Walk along the branch road past the houses and on the track to the beach, crossing a causeway over a small stream. Continue along the sand at first and then on the edge of the machair outside the fenced area. This is so that you do not accidentally pass the end of the fenced land where a faint but wide track leads across the machair to the other side of the peninsula. When some cultivated ground is reached bear left over the dunes to see the long stretch of sands, Tràigh Iar, which end at Veilish Point.

Before reaching Huilish Point there are some old walls on the headland, and the excavated site of Udal lies inland from these on a small hillock. Follow the coast by Tràigh Udal and on up to the trig point on Aird a' Mhòrain to enjoy the views. Cross the headland behind to the east side to reach the mausoleum of the Macleans of Boreray. The author was surprised to find a cat living in a rabbit warren here, but was told by a local crofter that many cats live and survive in this way. They are not wild cats, just domestic animals which have found the teeming rabbit population provides a good living.

Return along the rough track or walk along the sand, crossing the sandspit of Corran Aird a' Mhòrain and rejoining the outward route.

**Note:** If the tide is exceedingly high, or for variety, a return can be made by the tractor track which begins at a gate about 200 m north of the causeway. This goes through a series of gates, then passes a ruined building and a walled field. After passing the field turn left along a grass strip leading to a gate and access to the narrow road to Sollas. From Sollas turn left along the main road back to the start. (This diversion adds 2 km to the walk.)

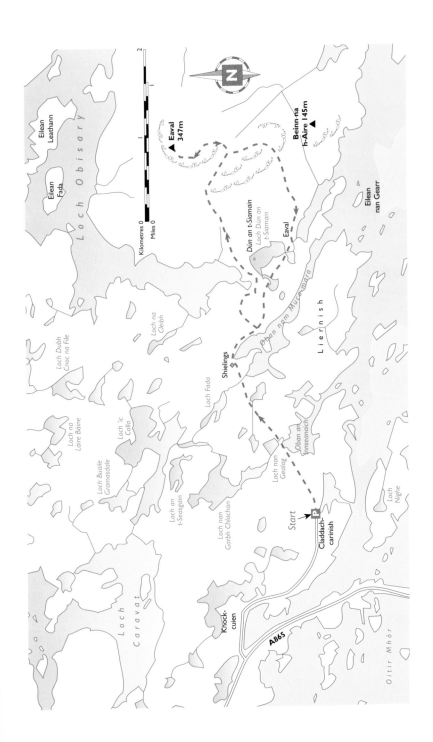

# EAVAL

A t 347 m, Eaval is the highest point of North Uist. Almost surrounded by water, the approach from any direction is circuitous. From Cnoc Cuien (spelt Knock-Cuien on the OS map and signposted on the ground as Knock Queen), it is something of an exercise in orienteering. In fact the walk in to the foot of the mountain takes longer than the ascent. Altogether it is a long and strenuous, but most rewarding experience which seasoned walkers will appreciate.

The easiest way to climb Eaval is from Loch Eport to the north, from where a well-trodden track can be followed, leading to the northeast ridge and returning the same way. On this approach, note that the outlet of Loch Obisary must be crossed on stepping stones which can be difficult, or even impossible, at high tide.

Parties who can arrange suitable transport can make a fine traverse of the mountain from Eport to Carinish. This traverse is used as an orienteering exercise by the Army and the author met numerous groups of trainees running from checkpoint to checkpoint. At the end of the day the officer in charge told me the fastest group had completed in less than two hours. Ordinary

## INFORMATION

**Distance:** 13 km (8 miles), with 370 m of climbing.

**Map:** OS Landranger sheet 22, Benbecula.

**Start and finish:** The road end at Claddach Carinish, GR 856589. Turn off the A865 3 km east of Carinish.

**Terrain:** Rough walking with only traces of path and very boggy in places. Boots and waterproofs essential. Take food and drink.

**Time:** 4–6 hours, depending on fitness and experience.

The start of the walk towards Eaval.

walkers are advised that in spite of its modest height, Eaval is a serious mountain and to make sure of an early start, especially in winter, when it is not unknown for people to be benighted.

The views from the top on a good day are quite outstanding, over an incredible wild landscape with lochs and lochans beyond counting scattered in the heather and peat moorland. Mountains galore abound in the 360-degree vista and it can take a considerable but enjoyable time to identify as many as you can.

**Note:** North Uist Estates request that all routes to Eaval are avoided in late June and early July when the deer are calving and also at stalking times in September and October.

Eaval.

From the wide parking area at the road end, take the track past an attractive thatched cottage. When the track ends continue in the same direction, aiming directly towards the summit of Eaval. There is boggy ground to contend with straight away, but with care it is possible to remain dryshod. This course brings you to the edge of a sea inlet (Oban an Innseanaich), which is followed to the left. Go through a gate and cross a little causeway, then bear left on a built-up path. Keep on the traces of path and make for a prominent cairn on a low hill which is a key landmark. From the cairn make for the next landmark which is a post on a hilltop, from where two ruined shielings at the head of a sea loch (Oban nan Muca-mara) can easily be seen and reached without too much effort.

From the second shieling, a fairly distinct path leads in a south-easterly direction around the edge of the sea loch. This goes through a gate and then continues in the same direction, crossing two narrow channels which are both branches of Loch Dùn an t-Siamain to arrive at the house called Eaval. From this point choose a way up on to the south ridge of Eaval.

The grassy gully on the left of a small but prominent bump on the ridge is a good place to aim for. Now turn left and follow the ridge to the top. This ridge is not as well defined as it appears from the approach route, but there are no difficulties. There is a distinct dip in the ridge at one point with some boggy ground to negotiate. Higher up, several cairns give the general direction.

To descend, return to the dip in the ridge and descend the grassy gully down towards Loch Obisary. When the angle eases, head towards two ruined shielings not shown on the map, but which stand out prominently from above. Cross the narrow strip of land between Loch Obisary and Loch Dun an t-Siamain. Keep near Loch Obisary to go through a gate, and then follow a path near the edge of the loch to a stile over a fence between Loch Obisary and a narrow unnamed loch.

Go along the north side of this loch and rejoin the outward route by the gate some ten minutes from the shielings at the head of the sea inlet. From the shielings return by the outward route, using the guidance of the hilltop post and the large cairn. Finally, the house at the road end comes into view and the return route is completed.

Looking north from Eaval.

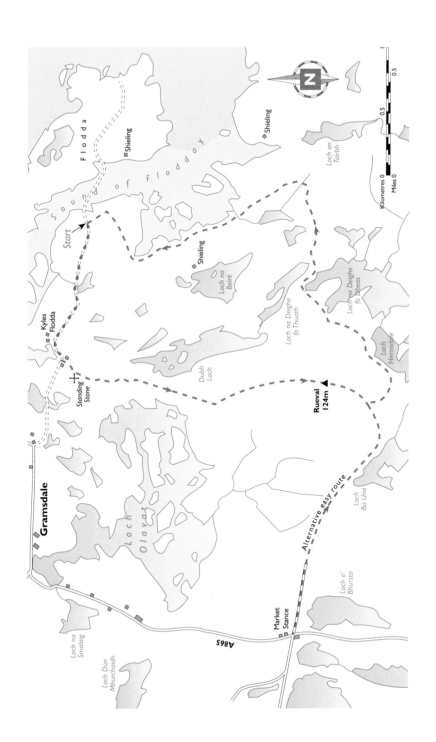

# RUEVAL

Before the causeways linking Benbecula were built (to South Uist in 1942 and to North Uist in 1963), the island was reached on foot or horseback by crossing sandy fords at low tide. The South Ford today is a popular place for local people to gather cockles in warm sunny weather. The crossing on foot is feasible from Creagorry on a track just past the Co-op, at low tide of course. On such days no one would suspect that the crossing had its hazards and even tragedies, usually because the short distance would tempt people across even when the tide had turned too far.

The North Ford was a much more perilous undertaking, following a long and tortuous route through several channels and tidal islets with quicksands either side to be avoided. At one time the route was marked on the map and there were cairns in the bay to mark the start. The main crossing was nearly 8 km in length, between the Carinish Inn at the head of Bàgh Mòr and Gramsdale on South Uist.

Although the crossing could be accomplished with ease in good weather and between the high spring tides, at other times there were deep channels to cross. The drovers who took cattle and ponies across could be up to their ribs in water, hanging on to the tail of the nearest animal. It was not unknown for a horse and trap to be lost, as happened to Father MacDougall, returning late at night from a sick call. Lucky enough to reach an islet, he was found the following evening with his hair turned white overnight. Think about this before attempting a crossing! If you are inspired to try, it would be advisable to seek a local guide.

Benbecula only measures 13 km by 10 km and is the lowest lying of all the islands, having only one hill, Rueval at 124 m. Because the surrounding land is so flat it provides a superb viewpoint, and its ascent is highly recommended. The all-round panorama presents a colourful scene on a sunny day with myriads

## INFORMATION

**Distance:** 9 km (5½ miles).

**Map:** OS Landranger sheet 22, Benbecula.

**Start and finish:** Park near the causeway over the Sound of Flodday (GR 839553), reached by taking the road east from the sharp corner (GR 820557) at Gramsdale on A865.

**Terrain:** Partly on road and track, partly pathless ground which is rough and boggy in places. Boots essential.

**Time:** About 3–3½ hours.

of bright blue lochans shining among the greens and yellows of grasses and the rich and varied shades of warm browns of the heather moors and peats. An attempt to count all the visible lochans from the top was made in 1824 by the writer J.MacCulloch, who had to give up after a count of 90. The hills of North Uist are conspicuous in the north-east and away to the south the bigger hills of South Uist tower over the intervening flat land and sea.

From the parking place, walk back along the narrow road past a small lochan, and after a bend left and another right go left, through a gate opposite a restored house. Make your way to a prominent Standing Stone, then continue along the rough moorland, heading almost due south. At first the going is rather tedious with many peat hags between patches of boggy ground, but this improves as you leave Loch Olavat and the Dubh Loch behind and begin rising up the gentle north ridge of Rueval.

Looking east from Rueval, showing the track.

Take your time at the top to appreciate the view to the full: it is an extraordinary and unique landscape laid out before you. When you are ready to leave, descend in a south-westerly direction to reach the broad track which comes in from Market Stance. Follow this track, much churned up by heavy vehicles, to the left as it curves round the foot of Rueval and crosses a narrow strip of land between Loch na Deighe fo Thuath and fo Dheas. Shortly afterwards take a left fork (the right fork leading to Loch Uiskevagh), the track now rising slightly over a low hill. Go through a gate on the brow of the hill and immediately turn left through a narrow gate. Aim for an old shieling at the side of a sandy bay on the west side of the Sound of Flodday.

From the shieling, an old path can be followed north for a little way. Then, if the tide is out, you can cut across the sand before reaching the final stretch of heather moor to return to the starting point.

If preferred, there is an easier option to reach the top of Rueval from Market Stance, which is at a crossroads on the A865 about 2 km south of Gramsdale. As its name implies, it was once the centre of the local economy, where stock was bought and sold, but today is the community refuse tip.

The track which heads east from here leads to Loch Uiskevagh and Rossinish on the east side of the island, possible destinations for other walks if time is available. For Rueval, drive along this track for about 800m to find a convenient parking place, then walk on until Loch Ba Una is passed and follow any of the narrow winding paths up to the top of the hill.

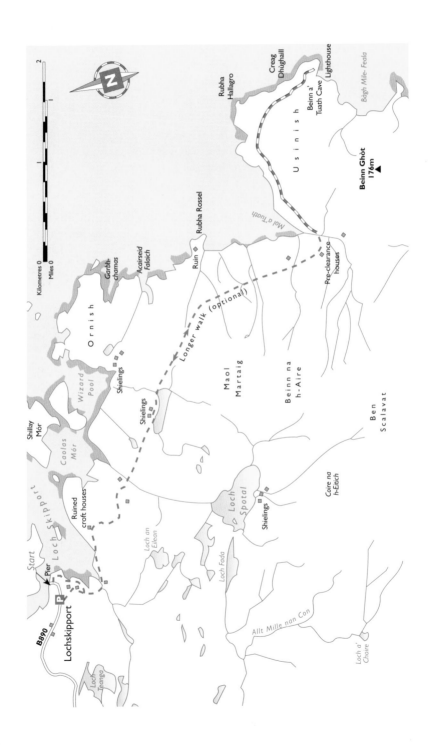

# LOCH SKIPPORT

This walk is the shortest in the book, but do not overlook it on that account. Historically and scenically, the area is of great interest and the walk can be extended at will according to your inclinations. The scenic drive along the B890 is most enjoyable, with views across Loch Druidibeg to the big hills of South Uist: Hecla, Ben Corodale and Beinn Mhor. Loch Druidibeg itself is a nature reserve of national importance with varying habitats of dunes, lochs and machair. A native flock of greylag geese nest on the islands in the loch and at one time the rare red-necked phalarope used to be sighted. The reserve extends to over 4000 acres and is administered by Scottish Natural Heritage.

Although some of the ruined houses in the area date from before the clearances, most are 20th century croft houses set up only when the Drimsdale farm was

## INFORMATION

**Distance:** 4 km (2½ miles).

**Map:** OS Landranger sheet 22, Benbecula.

**Start and finish:** From A865 on South Uist, turn off just north of Stilligarry onto B890 and follow it to its end. Park near the abandoned mailbox. The path starts above the ruined pier at Loch Skipport.

**Terrain:** Good path, although it is deteriorating and boots are advisable.

**Time:** Allow 1½–2 hours for the short walk, or much longer if you plan to explore.

Ruined crofthouse, Loch Skipport.

broken up in 1924. These crofts were gradually abandoned from the 1940s onwards, particularly when piped water and electricity became available in other areas of South Uist in the 1950s. Notice the old rigs or ploughmarks near the ruins and contemplate the harsh life and isolation of the people who lived here. Some of the ruins inland are shielings used in summer only when grazing animals, others by the coast were in use almost year-round when kelp was being worked.

Caolas Mòr.

Loch Skipport is popular with yachtsmen, being both sheltered and easily entered. The Shillay islands provide sheltered anchorage in either Caolas Mòr (wrongly known to yachtsmen as Little Kettle Pool), or Wizard Pool, which can be entered either by a narrow channel from Caolas Mòr or from the west. These pools can be seen by heading east from the ruined croft house where the built-up path ends and then following the coast round.

The views from the small hill above the ruins to which the path leads are truly panoramic. Across Loch Skipport, Ben Tarbert dominates the area of East Gerinish. Across the sea, features on Skye such as MacLeod's Tables are readily picked out on a good day. To the south, the attractive ridges and buttresses of Hecla catch the eye. Hillwalkers with sufficient time at their disposal will have no trouble picking out a route up the long curving ridge over Maol Martaig, Beinn na h-Aire and Ben Scalavat to the top. Another possibility for a longer exploration would be to try to follow the route to the lighthouse at GR 873350. A good 14 km round trip from the end of the decent path, this was once regularly walked by the postman three times each week.

Instead of taking the path from its starting point near the old mailbox, walk down to see the remains of the pier (driving down to the pier is not advised, as turning round is most awkward). This pier was erected in 1887 by Lady Gordon Cathcart for private use. After 1914 the pier came into general use, exporting cattle and sheep and importing such items as building materials and gas cylinders for South Uist.

Halfway down towards the pier, a narrow path begins on the right and follows the coastline round to join the main path by a stile. Follow this path round to the south side of Loch Skipport, passing several ruins. Two insignificant burns are crossed, all that remains of the bridges that once crossed them being the stone piers, inscribed with the date 1926. This path was built for the benefit of the children living in the then new crofting community.

The path passes below a house which is still intact, but ends at a ruined croft house standing above a swathe of yellow irises. The small island in Loch Skipport due north of this house is said to have been the site of a Viking castle. Go up the hill behind for the outstanding views, then explore the area as you wish before returning by the good path which leads to the mailbox.

Hecla from Loch Druidibeg.

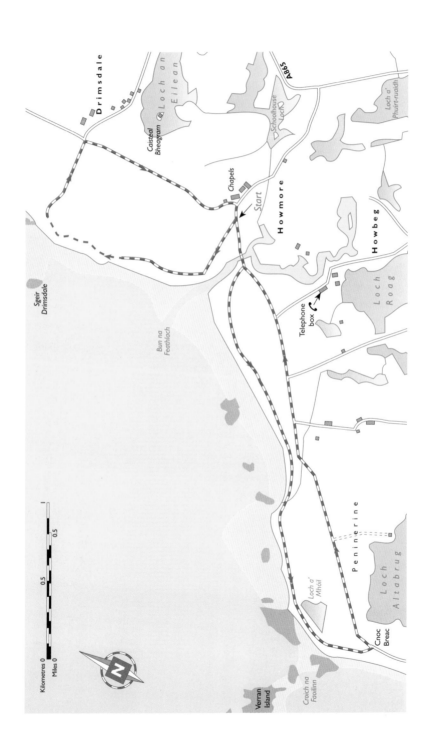

# TOBHA MOR (HOWMORE)

### INFORMATION

**Distance:** 10 km (6 miles).

**Map:** OS Landranger sheet 22, Benbecula.

**Start and finish:** Howmore church (GR 756364), reached by taking the signposted road to 'Howmore Chapel and Burial Ground' west from the A865.

**Terrain:** Easy walking on good paths and tracks. No special footwear needed.

**Time:** 2½–3 hours.

**Note:** There is some controversy over the correct Gaelic form of Howmore. It has been variously rendered as Tobha Mor, Tobha Mhor and t-Hogh Mor. We have used Tobha Mòr here for simplicity.

Howmore means 'big church' and is an interesting ecclesiastical site with the remains of two chapels and two churches of medieval origin, which were destroyed during the Reformation. The parish of Howmore was first mentioned in documents in the late 14th century. The largest building was Teampall Moire (St Mary's Church), measuring 20 m by 8 m, and this is the first to be reached as the site is approached. When built, it was the largest building in the Western Isles, but only the east gable is now standing.

The remains of the other buildings lie within a walled enclosure. One is Caibeal Dhiamaid, known as Father Dermot Duggan's church – he was a 17th century priest. Another is Caibeal Dubhghaill. Highest on the mound is Caibeal Clann ic Ailein, the chapel and burial ground of the Macdonalds of Clanranald, the chiefs from 1373 to 1838. It has been suggested that in its heyday, the cluster of buildings was a major centre of learning with an international reputation equal to that of Iona.

The site is thought to be a 'cashel', that is an area enclosed by walls or by ditches and banks, within which were churches or chapels and accommodation for clerics. A cashel was outside the law of the land so

Howmore ecclesiastical site.

that fugitives from local justice could claim sanctuary there. The wealth of the religious community was also stored in these cashels, and they were thus places that attracted the attention of Viking raiders. The churches were abandoned in the late 17th century, possible as a result of the great storm of 1697, which greatly altered the west coast of these islands. A site plan and description can be found in *The Ancient Monuments of the Western Isles* (HMSO, 1994).

Gatliff Trust hostel, Howmore.

Next to the ruins is a restored house which is run as a youth hostel by the Gatliff Trust, who are also restoring two others nearby. Down the road are two more old houses which are still inhabited and which are now listed buildings. Once common, most of these thatched houses have been abandoned and fallen into disrepair, although a few have been modernised. A charity, Cairdean nan Tighean Tugha (the Friends of the Thatched Houses), helps to restore them when possible.

The described walk makes a figure of eight with two loops of 3.5 and 6.5 km (2 and 4 miles), either of which makes a satisfying shorter walk. There are fine sea views and also good views inland across to the high mountains of South Uist. Although the OS map is marked 'danger area' between Verran Island and Sgeir Drimsdale, this no longer applies, the southern limit of the Royal Artillery range being at GR 754398, just north of Grogarry Loch.

From the ruined churches, walk towards the sea on a wide track surfaced with beach pebbles. Go straight on at a T-junction and follow the sandy path north at the edge of the dunes. The path dwindles to nothing, but just keep walking on the edge of the machair with lovely sea views on the one side and the shapely hills of Hecla, Ben Corodale and Beinn Mhor rising above the moorland on the other.

Beinn Mhor from Howmore track.

When the rocks of a skerry, Sgeir Drimsdale, are seen forming a rocky point in the sea, turn inland on an indefinite track through crofting land. Keep to one of the grassy strips between the ploughed areas. Turn right along a well-defined track which is met as the first houses of Drimsdale are seen.

As Loch an Eilean (loch of the island) is passed on the left, note the ruin on the small island. This is Caisteal Bheagram, a tower which measures 3.1 by 3.9 m internally and with walls 1.1 to 1.4 m thick. It is known to have been owned by Ranald Alansoun of Ylandbigrim in 1505. At Howmore, cut across some wet ground by a fence to reach the site of the old chapels behind the hostel.

To begin the second part of the walk, start towards the sea again and then bear left along a grassy path to the bridge. The river mouth is wide here and in days gone by, used to give shelter to fishing boats, one of the few safe anchorages on the west coast of South Uist. Cross the bridge and turn right along a sandy path by the dunes.

After just over 1 km the path almost joins the road, and anyone who wants to shorten the walk can do so here. Otherwise continue along the coast, here edged by a broad band of rocks, to reach Loch a Mhoil where there are usually some mute swans. A small rocky island, Verran Island, lies offshore. As the track swings inland to join the road, a Standing Stone can be seen ahead, but to reach this would add a further kilometre each way to the walk. Instead, follow the narrow lane back to Howmore.

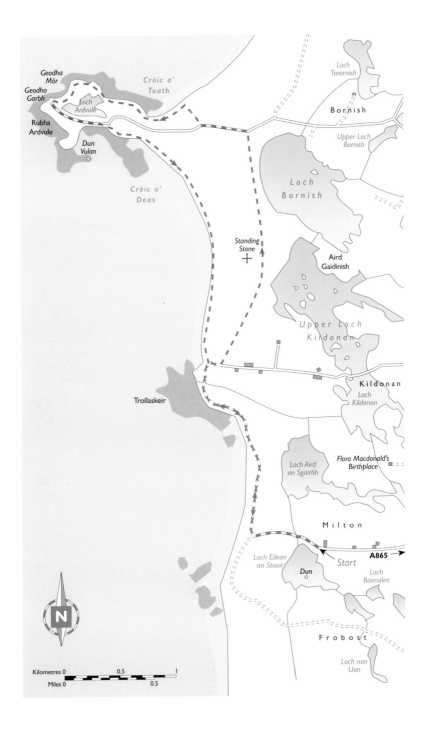

# RUBHA ARDVULE

This is a coastal walk with both fine views of sand and sea on the one hand and moors and hills on the other. Rubha Ardvule, said to be named after a Viking princess, is an interesting narrow headland with a freshwater lochan that is barely above the high water mark of the sea on either side. Many birds inhabit the loch and the bays on both side of the point. Expect to see eider duck among the oystercatchers and the gulls, and possibly a mute swan or two.

Another point of interest is the ruined fort, Dun Vulan, on the south side, where recent archaeological work has been carried out by Sheffield University. The machair in this area is unusual in including the red spikes of purple loosestrife, which is quite a rare plant in the Western Isles.

From the parking place, walk out towards the coast and turn right at a T-junction, following the sandy track northwards to Trollaskeir Point. You may see

The South Uist coast near Milton.

heaps of the deep-sea weeds laminaria or 'tangles' set up to dry on old telegraph poles or huge tree trunks, often supported on old oil drums. Presumably all these trees have been washed up by the sea, for no such trees grow in the area.

This type of seaweed on the west coast is normally collected between October and March, but it could be

## INFORMATION

**Distance:** 13 km (8 miles).

**Map:** OS Landranger sheet 22, Benbecula.

**Start and finish:** Milton, parking opposite the last house (GR 733263). From the A865 take the road west signposted Ghearaidh Bhailteas.

**Terrain:** Sandy tracks and paths, all easy walking.

**Time:** About 3½ hours.

**Note:** Part of this walk is in an area owned by the RA range, although at the time of writing (autumn 1995) it was not being used. Should it be used again in the future, the walk could not be done on firing days. Red flags are flown on these occasions and the sounds are unmistakable, but if in doubt enquire locally. There is no firing on Sundays.

Looking south-east from
near Dun Vulan.

left as late as May. After preliminary drying, the tangle
is loaded onto lorries and shipped to Alginate
Industries at Girvan on the Ayrshire coast.

Another type of seaweed, rockweed or *ascophyllum*, is
collected on the east coast and partly processed on
Benbecula, this industry currently employing about 30
people. Both types of seaweed are used to produce a
chemical which has the properties of jelling,
thickening and stabilising, and it has a wide range of
uses in food processing, textiles, paper, ceramics and
welding.

After a sharp right bend, turn left along a wide earth
path through partly cultivated croft land. There are
fine views across Upper Loch Kildonan and Loch
Bornish to the hills in the east. There is now no sign of
the Standing Stone marked on the OS map at the left
of the track: it has been buried by the encroaching
sand.

When, just past Loch Bornish, a rough but metalled road is met at a T-junction with a football field on the corner, turn left. Keep on the road for about 400 m and then cross over to the edge of the dunes on the north side. Walk along by the coast and then cross the narrow strip of land separating Loch Ardvule from the sea. Right at the end of the headland there is a trig point with a viewing platform overlooking the sea, where breakers foam over the rocks.

Turn left and follow the rough road along the south side of the loch, passing Dun Vulan. Leave the road to walk along the grassy edge of the dunes all the way back to Trollaskeir. Low fences have to be stepped over in two places. From Trollaskeir, follow the track back to Milton.

Freshwater loch on Rubha Ardvule.

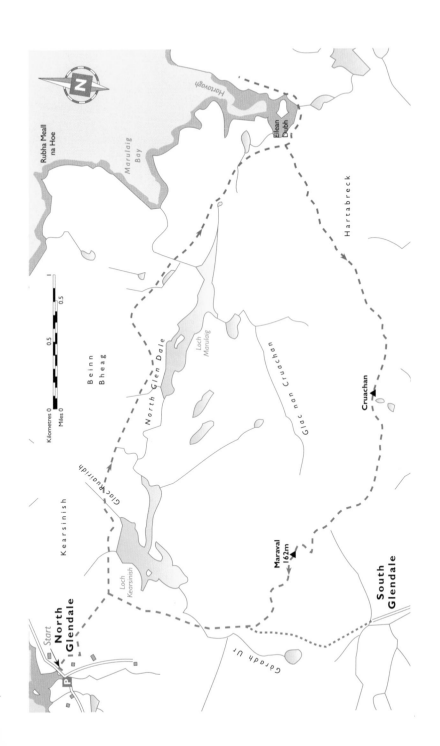

# NORTH GLENDALE AND HARTAVAGH

This walk explores a remote area south of Loch Boisdale, making use of two good moorland tracks. One goes through North Glendale and leads to a number of abandoned croft houses at Bagh Hartavagh. The houses at Hartavagh were built when the big sheep farm of Kilbride was broken up in 1907, but they were abandoned in 1927. During the years of occupation there were six children in the small community who used to walk along the track to the school, which was halfway between Hartavagh and North Glendale.

The return route is a hill walk over Hartabreck, Cruachan and Maraval, joining the track from South to North Glendale for the final stretch. The hill walking is straightforward but moderately strenuous.

Walk along the narrow coast road for about 150 m and then turn right up a grassy ramp to a wicket gate by a footpath sign. When a fence is met across the path turn right, following a right of way sign. At the end of the fence, turn left, uphill, to reach a wide gate giving access to the open fell. Continue uphill on a vague path going roughly south-east.

## INFORMATION

**Distance:** 12 km (7½ miles), with 385 m of climbing.

**Map:** OS Landranger sheet 31, Barra and surrounding Islands.

**Start and finish:** North Glendale. Take A865 to Daliburgh, B888 south for 4 km and then turn left onto the road signposted to South Lochboisdale. Park at the road end just past a new bungalow.

**Terrain:** Some well defined paths which are boggy in places. Pathless but easy walking on the hills. Boots essential.

**Time:** Allow 4–4½ hours.

Broken bridge, North Glendale track.

Ignore the wheelmarks leading right, but turn right a little further on along a grassy path. This leads to an area where peats are cut. On the shoulder of the hill the path becomes better defined and begins to contour the slopes of Kearsinish, above the loch of the same name where there is a fish farm.

Fish farming is making a real contribution to the economy of the Western Isles after its introduction in the 1970s. The salmon eggs have to be hatched in fresh water, as here in Loch Kearsinish. The young are then grown through the stages of fry, parr and smolt, at which stage they are transferred to other fish cages in sheltered seawater. If you are doing this walk in April or May you may see a helicopter flying between the tanks in Loch Kearsinish and some in Loch Boisdale, with a load of smolt dangling below.

The good track continues through the wide glen which is all heather and coarse grass, with a few violets the only flowers in early May, to be followed by orchids in June and July. Towards the end of Loch Marulaig the track crosses the burn by a kind of causeway, on the right of what used to be a substantial bridge, once of great benefit to the school children who had to walk this track in all weathers during the time that Hartavagh was occupied. The track continues to the head of Hartavagh and around it, with views of Eilean Dubh and of seacliffs below the rocky top of Meall an Iasgaich.

Just before reaching Hartavagh, a line of old fence posts points in the direction of the top of Hartabreck. Boggy at first, the going is good higher up on dry grass, heather and rocky outcrops. There are fine views back over Meall an Iasgaich and out over the sea to Skye and Rum. From Hartabreck, go over a shallow depression to Cruachan – the name echoing a rather better-known mountain on the mainland – which has two small lochans on its long ridge-like top. Here the eye is drawn to Eriskay and Barra.

Follow the ridge down and then turn north for the short descent and final rise to Maraval (162 m).

Top: Hartavagh from Hartabreck.

Above: Across North Glendale from Hartabreck.

Descend anywhere on the west slopes to join the path from South Glendale, and so back to the starting point. Although this track is well made, it does go through some flat and waterlogged areas before the rise up to the path junction. Take great care as it is easy to step into deep bog in places.

Walkers with time in hand might like to add a short diversion to the top of Roneval, a 201 m top overlooking the Sound of Eriskay. A shapely peak, steep on all sides except the north-east by which is it approached, it is a fine viewpoint. From the col between Hartabreck and Cruachan, contour south-west, then south, to the col between Cruachan and Roneval, from where there is a short ascent of about 80 m to reach the top.

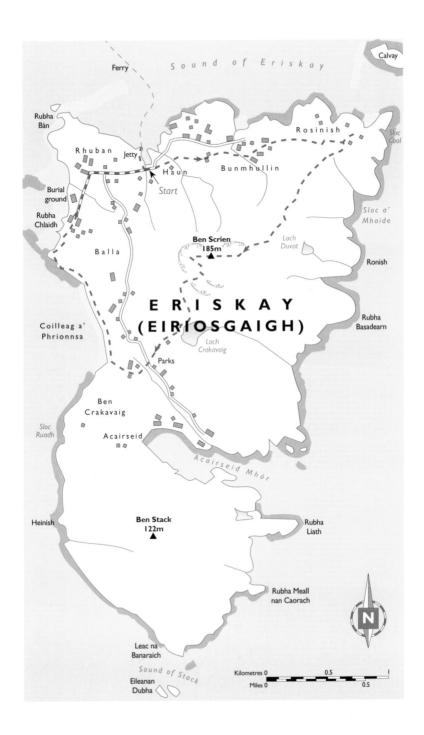

Calvay

Ferry

*Sound of Eriskay*

Rubha
Bàn

R h u b a n   Jetty

Rosinish

*Sloc
Caol*

Haun   B u n m h u l l i n

*Start*

Burial
ground

Rubha
Chlaidh

*Sloc a'
Mhaide*

B a l l a

**Ben Scrien**
**185m**
▲

*Loch
Duvat*

Ronish

**E R I S K A Y**
**(E I R I O S G A I G H)**

Coilleag a'
Phrionnsa

*Loch
Crakavaig*

Rubha
Basadearn

Parks

Ben
Crakavaig

*Sloc
Ruadh*

Acairseid

*A c a i r s e i d   M h ó r*

Heinish

**Ben Stack**
**122m**
▲

Rubha
Liath

Rubha Meall
nan Caorach

N

Leac na
Banaraich

*Sound of Stack*

Eileanan
Dubha

Kilometres 0                    0.5                    1
Miles 0                                      0.5

# ERISKAY: BEN SCRIEN

The romantic island of Eriskay (Eiriosgaigh) has several claims to fame. One is the silver sand beach on the west side, which was the first point of landing on Scottish soil for Bonnie Prince Charlie at the start of the 1745 rebellion. Another is more recent, when the SS Politician went down in 1941 with a cargo which included 20,000 cases of whisky. This shipwreck, and the hilarious events which followed, were immortalised by Compton Mackenzie in his novel *Whisky Galore*.

I was told that even today, caches of whisky are still being found, having been hidden or buried by people who are no longer alive. Now the name has been used for a pub opened in 1988, where relics of the SS Politician are on display. The pub is not open all day, so if you want to visit, you must be there at lunchtime.

During the infamous clearances the population of Eriskay 'exploded' from 80 in 1841 to 405 in 1851. This is because the island was considered too barren to support sheep, so there was an influx of people driven from their homes elsewhere. It was a hard struggle for so many to make ends meet and the population gradually declined.

Today there is a population of about 200, making a living from fishing and crofting. The crofts are small and most money is earned by fishing, mainly for crabs and lobsters, which are shipped to Spain from Ludag. Two larger vessels fish the Minch.

## INFORMATION

**Distance:** 9 km (5½ miles).

**Map:** OS Landranger sheet 31, Barra and surrounding Islands.

**Start and finish:** Jetty on North Eriskay. Several ferries each day ply between Eriskay and Ludag on the south coast of South Uist. Because the water in the Sound of Eriskay is shallow, the tides sometimes dictate that the last ferry leaves Eriskay at 1600 or earlier, so be sure to check with the ferryman before starting the walk.

**Terrain:** Some easy walking on paths and tracks, but the way over Ben Scrien is pathless and boots are advised.

**Time:** 3–3½ hours.

**Refreshments:** Am Politician, 1230 to 1430, all year round. Snacks at the Community Hall, next to the school, summer only.

Looking north from Ben Scrien on Eriskay.

A few crofters still keep Eriskay ponies, a breed originally kept for carrying peats and seaweed, but now more in demand for use in riding schools. The Eriskay pony is a rare breed, once almost in danger of extinction, but now being bred in the pure form by a preservation society and other interested individuals. The foals are born black but grow up white or grey.

Eriskay also has a strong Gaelic culture including folk songs and most people have heard of the Eriskay Love Lilt, even though they may only have a hazy idea of where Eriskay is.

Like most of the islands, Eriskay has abundant wild flowers in spring and summer including rare orchids, with some 60 species of plants in the machair. An unusual one is the pink sea convolvulus, said to have been introduced by the Prince himself. Skylarks and wheatears inhabit the high ground, and buzzards and hen harriers may be seen. Walkers are welcome to roam but are expected to leave gates as they are found and to keep dogs under close control. At 185 m, Ben Scrien is the highest point of this small island which measures only 5 km by 3 km. The ascent is quite easy and well worth while for the outstanding views.

Go up the road from the jetty and turn left at the T-junction. Almost immediately take a right fork along an old grass track which passes a telephone box. Fork left at another junction on an old built-up track. When this meets the road, cross it and continue past a new house and through a gate. The old track leads to Rosinish where there are a number of ruined houses on a grassy headland. Step over a low fence for access to this area, which makes a satisfactory destination for anyone wanting a shorter walk.

To continue, follow the low fence to the right and pass the prominent ruin at the head of a burn. Then make your way up the broad and grassy spur which extends from Ben Scrien to Rosinish. Although this is not as simple as it looks on the map, the top is visible nearly all the way and there are no real difficulties. Find the easiest but somewhat meandering way up grassy slopes with some inevitable ups and downs, keeping in a generally south-westerly direction. A small loch, Loch Duvat, is seen below on the left.

Barra from Ben Scrien, Eriskay.

As might be expected, the views from the top are truly panoramic, with South Uist to the north and Barra to the south-west. In sunny weather the sea colours are superb, a mixture of palest turquoise where the water lies over sand, and deep violet and indigo where there are seaweed-covered rocks beneath.

To descend, head west for a short distance then zig-zag down grassy slopes to the south. Look out for a gate in the fence which runs down a shallow valley towards Loch Crakavaig and go down a long grassy gully to reach this. Turn left and go down to the loch where some peat cuttings will be seen. Pass to the right of a small reservoir and head down towards the road at Coilleag.

Cross the road and go over a wide bridge over a small burn. Pass between the houses and over a grassy col towards a gate. Ignore the gate and go to the left of it to pick up a path leading north at the back of the Prince's beach (Coilleag a' Phrionnsa). Either walk along this path or go down onto the sand to the far end, where a pleasant grassy path leads round a point, Rubha Chlaidh, on which there is a golf course. At Balla, the path joins a narrow road which passes 'Am Politician', then turns right. Keep straight on at the junction by the school and then turn first left to return to the jetty.

Eriskay jetty.

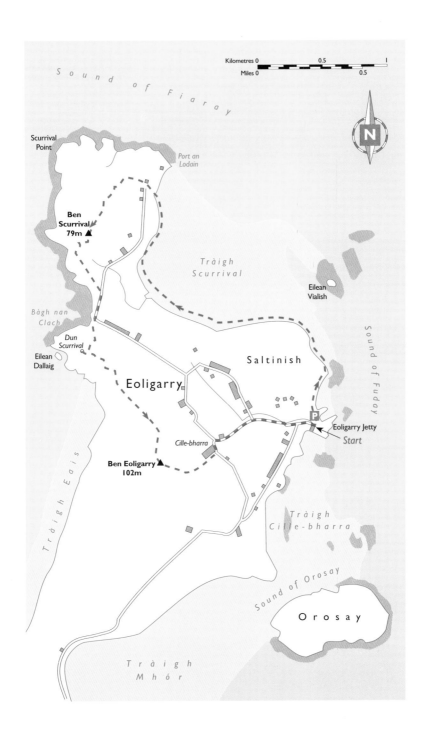

# BEN SCURRIVAL AND BEN EOLIGARRY

At the northernmost point of Barra, past the airfield on the vast expanse of firm sand at Traigh Mhor (big beach) is a small peninsula which provides a walk of surprising variety, partly on sand and partly on hill and moor. Two sites of great historical interest are also visited.

The first, Dun Scurrival, is an Iron Age fort perched on a low hilltop close to the west coast and overlooking the long sandy bay of Traigh Eais to the south. There are many hundreds of these duns (some are called brochs) throughout the Hebrides, often sited on rocky points and hilltops which offer some degree of protection from potential attackers. Often, as in this case, little remains to be seen of the construction except a tumbled circular wall around a grassy hollow. Originally it was a galleried structure with a space between the inner and outer walls.

The one thing they all have in common is a fine view, and Dun Scurrival is no exception. Duns were among the first walled buildings to appear in Scotland, from the 7th century BC onwards. Other duns in the area are Dun Ban on the way to Doirlinn Head (Walk 24) and a ruined dun on Vatersay (Walk 25).

The second interesting site is Cille Bharra, which dates from the Norse period in the 12th century. It is

## INFORMATION

**Distance:** 8 km (5 miles).

**Map:** OS Landranger sheet 31, Barra and surrounding Islands.

**Start and finish:** The parking area at Eoligarry jetty. To reach this take A888 east then north from Castlebay and at Northbay take the turnoff signposted to Eoligarry. After passing the airstrip, take the next right turn. The jetty may also be reached by a small passenger ferry from Ludag in South Uist. Enquire locally for times.

**Terrain:** Easy walking on firm sand and then open moorland, although this is pathless and boggy in places. Boots advisable.

**Time:** 2½–3 hours.

**Refeshments:** At the Airport terminal (summer only).

**Toilets:** At the Eoligarry jetty carpark.

Eoligarry.

thought the church might have been built on even older foundations, possibly from the 7th century, i.e. before the Viking invasion by Onund Wooden-Leg, who landed on Barra in 871. Cille Bharra contains a replica of a rune stone found in the churchyard in 1865. The stone is 1.4 m high and a translation of the runes is 'After Thorgerth, Steiner's daughter, this cross was raised'.

Eoligarry is one of the many places on Barra where the machair is dominated in early summer by primroses which form a dense yellow carpet. At this time of the year a surprising number of wild flowers are yellow; gorse, broom, lesser celandine and marsh marigold spring to mind, but there always violets here and there too. Eoligarry is also one of the places where you may be lucky enough to see a corncrake.

Once common, the corncrake is almost extinct in Britain due to mechanisation of harvesting. In the Western Isles the meadows are harvested later, and there is also much uncultivated ground, and this allows the corncrakes a chance to breed. They often take cover in patches of irises (yellow flags) and are notoriously difficult to spot, but their characteristic rasping call is frequently heard in mid May or early June.

All the land on Barra is held as crofter's smallholdings, and there are no large farms. In 1901, 3000 acres of Eoligarry farm were bought by the Congested Districts Board and were used to create 58 much-needed holdings for crofters. The remainder of the farm was settled on by crofters after the first World War in 1919. The land is good grazing and several breeds of cattle are raised. Sheep were not introduced until about 1839, mostly Scottish blackfaced whose wool goes to Lewis for the Harris Tweed industry. Walkers are welcomed but requested to avoid crops and always to close gates.

Ben Scurrival from Ben Eoligarry.

From the jetty, walk north along the shell sand beach, richly strewn with a variety of shells. Look out for Arctic terns which breed here as well as the more common ringed plovers, redshanks and dunlin. Across a narrow strip of water to the east is Fuday island, with Eriskay beyond.

Keep walking right round the bay (Traigh Scurrival) until a narrow wooden gate is seen at the top of a grassy bank. Go through this and cross the field to another gate on the right of a cottage. Go through this gate too and then turn half right to a third gate, then half left on an indistinct path which leads to two more gates. Continue towards a fence passing a tiny lochan, then make for the top of Ben Scurrival by easy slopes.

After enjoying the view to the full, continue down the south side of the hill and after crossing some lazybeds, make for a gate on to the road. Follow this to a corner; where the road makes a sharp left turn, keep straight on up grassy slopes to Dun Scurrival. More lazybeds are seen on the way across the broad ridge and on up to the top of Ben Eoligarry (102 m).

Replica of rune stone, Cille Bharra.

Once on the top, turn left along a dyke and then down a grass slope to reach a gate on the road at the right-hand side of the cemetery. The reproduction of the rune stone, which has a Celtic cross on the back, is housed in the north chapel, which has been re-roofed for this purpose. The original is in the National Museum of Antiquities in Edinburgh. The chapel also houses the late medieval carved tombstones found in the graveyard. For more information on this site see *The Ancient Monuments of the Western Isles* (HMSO, 1994). From the cemetery, walk along the lane to return to the jetty.

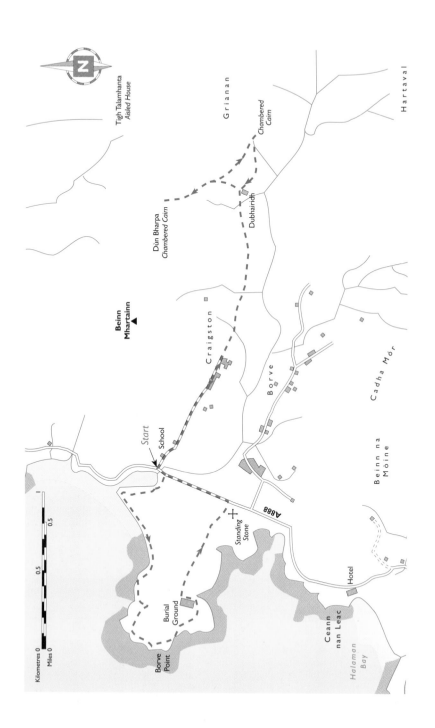

# BORVE POINT AND DÙN BHARPA

**INFORMATION**

**Distance:** 9½ km (6 miles).

**Map:** OS Landranger sheet 31, Barra and surrounding Islands.

**Start and finish:** The large parking area opposite the Craigston road end, 5 km (3 miles) north from Castlebay.

**Terrain:** Easy walking but mainly pathless and boggy in places. Boots advisable.

**Time:** 3–3½ hours.

**Refreshments:** The Isle of Barra Hotel at Tangasdale is near the start.

Borve Point, on the west coast of Barra, is a flat, grassy headland between two fine sandy bays, enclosed by Greian Head to the north and Doirlinn Head to the south. There are fine views of hills and sea, with white surf breaking over the rocky foreshore in the foreground. Gulls, oystercatchers, ringed plovers, lapwings and larks abound and the sheep-cropped turf is a delight to walk on.

The second part of the walk heads inland to visit two chambered cairns. One of these, Dùn Bharpa, is situated on a col at 130 m between Beinn Mhartainn and Grianan. Although collapsed, it is still impressively large, being 26 metres in diameter. There was an inner chamber with a roof slab measuring 3 m by 2 m, similar to that of Barpa Langass on North Uist which is better preserved. At Dun Bharpa some of the surrounding upright standing stones are still in place. The site was probably used as a communal burial chamber.

From the carpark walk back across the bridge and turn right by the school sign to gain access to the headland. Either walk on the sand or on the edge of

Approaching Borve Point.

the dunes, following the coastline west and keeping outside the fenced area. At one point a side fence extends to the edge of the grass and must be stepped round somewhat awkwardly, or the stones on the foreshore negotiated instead.

When a deep gully cuts across the headland, make a slight detour inland and then continue all the way round on the grassy turf. When the burial ground is reached, go round it on the right to join the track leading back to the road. The Borve Standing Stone, the visible height of which is only about a metre, is found on the right just before reaching the road. Turn left to complete the first part of the walk.

Cross back over the bridge and turn right, passing the school and going through the small township of Craigston. The surfaced road soon ends and a wide track continues up the glen to end by an old thatched house. As this is approached, the site of the second cairn can be seen clearly above and beyond the house, on an oasis of bright green grass. The house is called the Dubharaidh (the dark shieling, also called the Thatched Cottage) and is open to visitors in the summer months.

Dun Bharpa.

When the house is reached, turn left through an old gate and go uphill outside the fence, picking the best way through the sloping field to avoid the boggy places. There is a good stile over the fence immediately opposite Dùn Bharpa. Descend partway towards the gate and then strike across the hillside to reach the other chambered cairn. This is an elongated site with traces of small shelters surrounding the central cairn. It is in a fine situation in a broad corrie embraced by the slopes of Hartaval and Grianan. A rough path over the bealach links Craigston with Earsairidh (Earsary) in the east. Return down the valley to reach the gate giving access to the track and walk back to the starting point.

This area can also be visited during the course of a long walk of 14 km from Castlebay over some of the highest tops of Barra. In clear weather this walk gives splendid views of the whole island and across the sea, west to the distant cliffs of St Kilda and east to the peaks of the mainland, as well as the nearby islands.

Heaval is climbed first by following the hill road up the Glen until it peters out, then striking up the steep but easy south-west slopes to reach the 'Lady Star of the Sea', a marble statue of the Virgin Mary erected in 1954 by the Welcome Home Fund for Seamen to mark the Marian Year of the Catholic Church. It stands at about 280 m. Continue up to the top of Heaval (383 m) and then go north across a low saddle to a second top.

The route now descends fairly steeply by the north ridge to the narrow Beul a' Bhealach. Grianan is reached by a moderate pull up the grassy slopes of a ridge trending roughly north-west. Although the walk can be extended northwards from Grianan to take in Cora-bheinn and Ben Verrisey, most walkers will be content to complete the round by making for Dun Bharpa next, then continuing up easy slopes to the top of Beinn Mhartainn. After dropping down to the coast road near the school, there is a walk of 5 km back to Castlebay.

Chambered cairn at GR 676 013

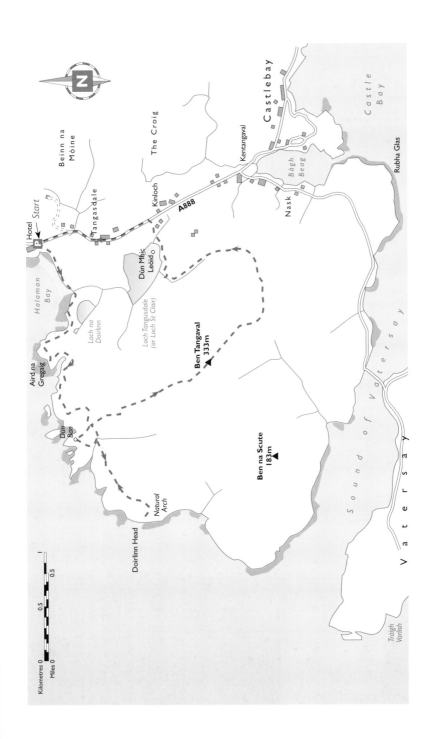

Kilometres 0    0.5    1
Miles 0    0.5

Halaman Bay

Hotel
Start
P

Aird na Gregaig

Dùn Bàn

Loch na Doirlinn

Dùn Mhic Leòid

Loch Tangusdale
(or Loch St Clair)

Natural Arch

Doirlinn Head

Ben Tangaval
333m

Ben na Scute
183m

Beinn na Mòine

Tangasdale

Kinloch

A888

The Croig

Kentangaval

Castlebay

Castle Bay

Bàgh Beag

Nask

Rubha Glas

Sound of Vatersay

Vatersay

Tràigh Varlish

# DOIRLINN HEAD

The white sand of Halaman Bay backed by sand dunes makes a delightful start to this interesting walk, which can be made either shorter or longer, according to inclination. The shorter version returns from Dun Ban, a ruined hillfort thought to be pre-Viking in origin, and the longer version for keen hillwalkers goes to the top of Ben Tangaval either by the north ridge or the northwest ridge, descending by a col south-east from the top and then down to Loch Tangusdale.

There are glorious views on a sunny day whichever version you choose, particularly looking north over Borve Point, and near at hand along the dramatic rocky coast with many small coves and inlets.

A stile from the hotel grounds gives access to Halaman Bay. Cross the curving edge of the sand to the other side and find a place to cross the small burn by a rocky outcrop. Turn right and follow the coast on green turf and slabby rocks. After going through a gate, make for some cairns on a patch of high ground, then turn inland to pass an inlet. Traces of a path are found. Continue following the edge of the land, making for a prominent cairn on the next broad headland. At this point Dun Ban can be seen ahead, but cannot be reached by a direct route because of intervening gullies and cliffs.

Instead, turn inland at right angles to the direct line and follow some

## INFORMATION

**Distance:** 6 km (4 miles).

**Map:** OS Landranger sheet 31, Barra and surrounding Islands.

**Start and finish:** Isle of Barra Hotel, Tangasdale, 3 km (2 miles) north of Castlebay on A888.

**Terrain:** Firm sand, grassy paths and some pathless moorland. Boots advisable if you go beyond Dun Ban.

**Time:** 2–2½ hours.

**Refreshments:** Served all day at the Isle of Barra Hotel.

Dun Ban.

cairns along a rocky bluff. When a grassy valley is reached, cross it by a kind of causeway and continue straight ahead, up a triangular grassy slope. Follow the same line up to a low col and descend slightly to meet a fence. Turn right and follow the fence to a gateway where the rusty gate has been replaced by a low fence, easily stepped over. Now turn right and follow the fence down to reach Dun Ban.

Dun Ban (white fort) is in a well-defended position with steep cliffs on three sides. Although in ruins, parts of the original structure can be identified, including a circular wall some 9 or 10 metres in diameter on the highest point, some ruined shelters and lower down part of a double wall. A curious feature is that all the stones are covered with a thick growth of thrift plants, just beginning to flower in early May.

Leave the fort and cross the headland to reach a deep gully where fulmars nest on the vertical walls. Those who wish to shorten the walk can now follow the gully inland to reach the step-over fence in the gateway.

Doirlinn Head.

To continue the walk to Doirlinn Head, walk towards this gateway but at the place where the gully makes a sharp bend, cross it and continue along the headland at roughly the same height until an amazing 'devil's cauldron' is reached. Here black, wet, vertical cliffs surround a deep hole where the sea pounds away below, making some terrifying noises.

It is necessary to retreat slightly and go above this frightening hole – and well away from the edge of it too. All is surprisingly easy walking and a kind of path can be found in places. Continue until you have rounded the corner and another headland can be seen across a bay. Now descend back right towards the cliffs, approaching the edge with caution, to view the splendid cliff scenery of Doirlinn Head.

Return by roughly the same route, going up above the gaping cauldron and crossing the moorland easily to reach the gateway in the fence and following the outward route back to Halaman Bay.

Halaman Bay.

Those with a mind to climb Ben Tangaval can do so either by going up the north ridge from the gateway in the fence, or by following the broader northwest ridge from above Doirlinn Head. Although the top is only 333 m, an ascent by either of the ridges can give a strenuous excursion, with the reward of a fantastic view from the top.

Then go down to a broad 220 m col on the south-east side. From here the descent is steep but not difficult down a grassy gully. Go over a shoulder and down to Loch Tangusdale near the ruined tower. Pass round the end of a fence in the loch and then make towards the road to find a gate. Turn left and walk back to the hotel.

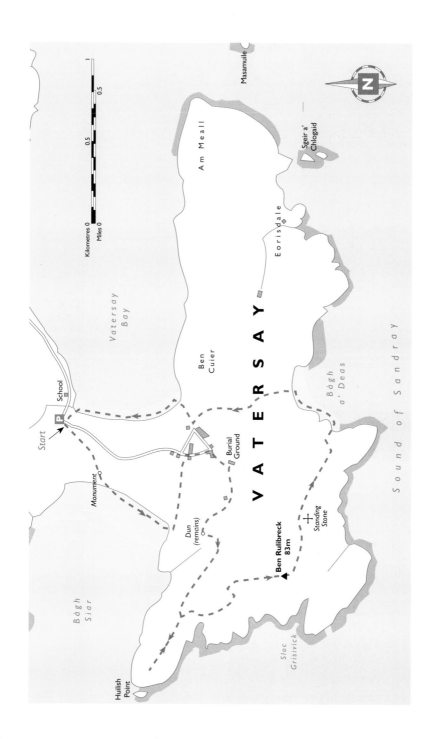

# VATERSAY: BEN RULIBRECK AND SOUTH BEACH

Until 1990, when a new causeway was built at a cost of £3 million, Vatersay was an island. The new road has ended some of the isolation for the islanders but has not detracted from the peaceful and quiet atmosphere of the place with its beautiful beaches of pale shell sand, dunes and flowering machair.

The beach on the west side was the scene of a tragic shipwreck in 1853, when the Annie Jane, bound for Quebec, foundered with the loss of 350 people. A granite monument erected in their memory stands on the dunes.

There was never a large population on the island and by 1901 the numbers had dwindled to 13. The Congested Districts Board, which had bought land at Eoligarry, bought 60 acres on Vatersay and divided it between 51 crofters. All should have been well, but the potato crops failed and there were various disputes unresolved when in 1907 several men from Castlebay landed on Vatersay and erected dwellings overnight, claiming possession of the land under an old Scottish law.

## INFORMATION

**Distance:** 8 km (5 miles).

**Map:** OS Landranger sheet 31, Barra and surrounding Islands.

**Start and finish:** Park on the grass where the road bends left to cross the waist of the island. To reach here drive west from Castlebay and take the third road to the left, signposted Bhatarsaigh. The new road is not on maps printed before 1990, but it crosses a low col and then hugs the coast before crossing the causeway to Vatersay.

**Terrain:** Sand, tracks, open moorland and grass, in places wet and boggy so boots advised.

**Time:** 2½–3 hours.

Huilish Point, Vatersay.

They were arrested and sentenced to six months in prison, but were released after serving two months. Their action helped to bring about changes to the law relating to crofting tenancies which are still valid today. The population is now 107 and is increasing since the causeway was built. Some new houses have been built in recent years.

From Ben Rulibreck there are splendid views over the sea to several smaller islands: Sandray, Pabbay and Mingulay.

Go over the stile at the edge of the machair on the west of the road and cross it to reach the monument. Go down to the beach and walk south along the firm sand, only covered when the tide is high. At the end of the beach go up the bank at the end and turn left, following the path into the village. At a T-junction by a telephone box, turn right and then right again through a field gate between two new houses.

Go towards the large derelict building, the remains of Vatersay House which was built in the 19th century as the tacksman's house when the island was owned by the Gordons of Cluny. On the left there is a gap in the fence next to a walled field. Bear right to the hill top on which there is a ruined dun. This is an excellent viewpoint, although there is little to be seen of the original structure owing to quarrying for building stone. There are much better preserved duns such as Dun Ban (Walk 24) and Dun Scurrival (Walk 22).

Descend left (south) to a stile in the fence and go through the gap between the Dun and the north top of Ben Rulibreck. Walk along the broad headland to a cairn above Huilish Point. The grass may be brown and coarse but pale yellow primroses push their way through in May. There are many outcrops of Lewisian gneiss, here with wavy stripes in grey and pink.

Return along the broad ridge for about 400 m and then drop down right to cross a broken fence at the head of a gully where there are some impressive rock formations. The north top of Ben Rulibreck is now

Standing stone (used as gateway).

easily reached by going up grassy slopes to the right of the top and then back left. Continue over a low col to reach the south top (83 m).

At this point, change direction and follow the high ground to the south-east. Aim for the prominent Standing Stone, about 2 m high, when it comes into view. Although probably Bronze Age in origin, it has later been incorporated into an enclosure wall as a kind of gatepost (GR 628949). It is not marked on the 1:50,000 OS map.

Continue going down towards the south beach (Bagh a' Deas), keeping outside the fenced area, which is carpeted with primroses. Access to the beach is by a stile between the fence and a deep gully. Walk along the beach and turn inland to pick up a track leading into the small township. On the edge of the village, turn right at a T-junction and walk along the east coast beach back to the starting point.

South Bay (Bàgh à Deas).

# INDEX

Opposite: Toe Head from Beinn Shleibhe.

Other titles in this series

25 Walks – In and Around Aberdeen
25 Walks – The Cotswolds
25 Walks – Deeside
25 Walks – Dumfries and Galloway
25 Walks – Edinburgh and Lothian
25 Walks – Fife
25 Walks – In and Around Glasgow
25 Walks – Highland Perthshire
25 Walks – The Scottish Borders
25 Walks – The Trossachs
25 Walks – The Yorshire Dales

Other titles in preparation

25 Walks – In and Around Belfast
25 Walks – The Chilterns
25 Walks – Fermanah

Long distance guides published by HMSO

The West Highland Way – Official Guide
The Southern Upland Way – Official Guide

**HMSO Bookshops**
71 Lothian Road, Edinburgh EH3 9AZ
0131-479 3141 Fax 0131-479 3142
49 High Holborn, London WC1V 6HB
(counter service only)
0171-873 0011 Fax 0171-831 1326
68–69 Bull Street, Birmingham B4 6AD
0121-236 9696 Fax 0121-236 9699
33 Wine Street, Bristol BS1 2BQ
0117 9264306 Fax 0117 9294515
9-21 Princess Street, Manchester M60 8AS
0161-834 7201 Fax 0161-833 0634
16 Arthur Street, Belfast BT1 4GD
01232 238451 Fax 01232 235401
The HMSO Oriel Bookshop, The Friary, Cardiff CF1 4AA
01222 395548 Fax 01222 384347

HMSO publications are available from:

**HMSO Publications Centre**
(Mail, fax and telephone orders only)
PO Box 276, London SW8 5DT
Telephone orders 0171-873 9090
General enquiries 0171-873 0011
(queuing system in operation for both numbers)
Fax orders 0171-873 8200

**HMSO's Accredited Agents**
(see Yellow Pages)

*and through good booksellers*

Printed in Scotland for HMSO by CC No. 70343 50c 7/96